focus

Into this one little book Lovett Weems has packed the fruit of years of loving, critical examination of our church. I wish I had this book when I was beginning to be bishop. In direct, concise fashion, Lovett tells us the specific tasks we have before us if our beloved church is to have a future. With *Focus*, we have the gift of a strong, clear prescription for our present malaise.

—Will Willimon, Bishop, The North Alabama Conference of The United Methodist Church and author of *Bishop: The Art of Questioning Authority by an Authority in Question* (Abingdon, 2012)

Lovett is spot-on, fact-based, and thorough in his analysis, with a deep understanding of The United Methodist Church. It is well worth the read for pastors, lay leaders, and denominational leaders with practical strategies to reset the course of The United Methodist Church for the twenty-first century without losing our Wesleyan values.

—Bob Farr, Director of Congregational Excellence, Missouri Conference, and author of *Renovate or Die: 10 Ways to Focus Your Church on Mission* (Abingdon, 2011)

Once again Lovett Weems hits the mark with what has become his signature strengths as a writer and researcher: Penetrating reforms for The United Methodist Church, backed by objective quantitative data. As all of us face adaptive challenges in our church work, Lovett provokes the conversation by enabling us to face our current realities and grounding his suggestions in hard data. This is a must read for any of us serious about reform of the mainline church.

—Bishop Grant Hagiya, Pacific Northwest Conference

Often our successes are more limiting than our failures. They cause us to look for our future in our past, in the glory days of old when everything seemed brighter and better. It is important to remember, however, that success is forged through the complex combination of the gifts, skills, knowledge, and energy of the human and material resources we have, rather than compensating for those things we lack. Lovett Weems is challenging us to quit trying to drive into the future by staring into the rearview mirror. The future we create will build on our story thus far, but the time has come to write a new chapter about what we can do and who we can become instead of a fond remembrance of who we once were.

—Dan R. Dick, Director of Connectional Ministries, Wisconsin Annual Conference

Weems gives one of the best analyses and assessments for the general church, annual conferences, and local churches with strategic and practical changes that are essential in order to be sustainable into the future. A must-read for all leaders in The United Methodist Church today!

—Sally Dyck, Resident Bishop of Minnesota, The United Methodist Church

Lovett Weems has clearly stated the essential biblical and theological foundations, named the undeniable realities, and begun the necessary conversation for practical solutions to the challenges facing our church in the twenty-first century. This is a must-read for leaders on all levels of the church's work.

—Bishop Thomas J. Bickerton, Western Pennsylvania Conference

Other Abingdon Press Books by Lovett H. Weems Jr.

Bearing Fruit: Ministry with Real Results
(with Tom Berlin)

Church Leadership: Vision, Team, Culture, and Integrity
Revised Edition

The Crisis of Younger Clergy
(with Ann A. Michel)

Take the Next Step: Leading Lasting Change in the Church

Leadership in the Wesleyan Spirit

John Wesley's Message Today

To subscribe to the free online newsletter of the Lewis Center for Church Leadership, *Leading Ideas*, go to www.churchleadership.com.

ADAPTIVE LEADERSHIP SERIES

focus

[The Real Challenges That Face
The United Methodist Church]

Lovett H. Weems Jr.

Abingdon Press
Nashville

focus

The Real Challenges That Face The United Methodist Church

This book is printed on acid-free paper.

Library of Congress Cataloging-in-Publication Data

Weems, Lovett H. (Lovett Hayes)
 Focus : the real challenges that face the United Methodist Church /
Lovett H. Weems, Jr.
  p. cm.
 Includes bibliographical references (p.   ).
 ISBN 978-1-4267-4037-4 (book - pbk. / trade pbk. : alk. paper) 1.
United Methodist Church (U.S.) I. Title.
 BX8382.2W44 2011
 287.6—dc23

                                                                    2011039749

11 12 13 14 15 16 17 18 19 20—10 9 8 7 6 5 4 3 2 1

MANUFACTURED IN THE UNITED STATES OF AMERICA

To

G. Douglass Lewis and David McAllister-Wilson,

Exemplary leaders, mentors, colleagues, and friends

Contents

Preface

Warren Pittman introduced me once as "a product of the church." When I was in high school, Warren was pastor in the Mississippi county-seat town where the school was located, and later, when I was a pastor, he was my district superintendent. My home church was part of a three-point charge out in the country, where I lived. Warren understood that for generations of youth whose worlds were very circumscribed by conventional standards, the church opened new worlds of ideas and opportunities.

I am deeply indebted to The United Methodist Church and proud of its monumental achievements, including those coming in the last generation, even amid numerical decline. The elimination of the Central Jurisdiction as a condition for union in 1968 opened a new chapter in the mixed history of race in the church. Only those most affected by this decision can appreciate the price paid by many to implement this historic action. Similarly, a generation of clergywomen has opened doors for a more inclusive and widespread place for all those called to ordained ministry. The church has been a pacesetter for society in more inclusive language. The ranks of top leadership positions have become far more diverse. Grassroots mission and spiritual formation initiatives have engaged thousands in expanding their discipleship horizons. Efforts to relieve suffering around the world have been exemplary. Thousands of lives have been touched in ways impossible to imagine were it not for The United Methodist Church.

So I write as a deeply grateful and proud product of the church with hope for a future that presents great challenges.

I also write out of the pragmatic tradition of our heritage. An example is the Christmas Conference of 1784 that, as Russell Richey notes, "established the precedent for the church's practice of shaping polity and policy guided by little in the way of biblical, theological, or other warrant."[1] Biblical, theological, and historical considerations matter greatly to me and have always been the foundation of my work; in this book, I put the focus on the practical manifestations of those commitments.

This book is for hopeful people yearning for the unfolding of God's new vision for the United Methodist witness in the United States. It is not a book about death, fear, or denominational survival, except to the extent that leaders ignore the signs of the times. God's work will move forward through the church universal with or without The United Methodist Church; but the distinctive Wesleyan witness in the United States represented by The United Methodist Church will be a part of God's work only through a closer alignment both to God and to the people in our midst.

I am fortunate to have the opportunity to work with people from every part of the denomination. I am certain we have much to learn from one another, whatever our callings within our church, and this book grows out of the generous gifts and wisdom shared by so many through the years. Its recommendations reflect the highest regard for all constituencies.

There will be much here for everyone both to like and to dislike. Focus on what you find worthy and useful, and the weaker ideas will fall away. It is my prayer that the conversation begun in these pages will continue in many corners of The United Methodist Church and thus bring us closer to that vision to which God is calling us in the days ahead.

The 1960s, the New York Yankees, and the Methodists

The year 1964 began as just another very good year for two of the venerable powerhouses of the twentieth century—the New York Yankees and The Methodist Church.

In each of their realms, the Yankees and the Methodists dominated the first half of the twentieth century. Year after year they were the major forces in the respective worlds of professional baseball and American Protestantism.

As the first of the baby boomers anticipated their high school graduation in the spring, the Yankees looked toward another round of spring training in Florida, and the Methodists prepared for their quadrennial General Conference in Pittsburgh. While baby boomers were ready to change the world based on their superior numbers and confidence, the Yankees and Methodists just wanted to "stay as good as we are" because, by conventional measures, they both had been very good for decades.

But things had not always been so good for either the Yankees or the Methodists.

The Road to the 1960s for the Yankees

The Yankees were not always winners. In 1912 they finished fifty-five games behind first place in the American League, worst in the history of the Yankees and one of the worst seasons by any team in the history of baseball. They set other ignoble historical records that year as well: lowest attendance, lowest percentage of wins at 33 percent, and lowest number of games won at fifty. But they changed owners in 1915 and quickly improved. In 1921, aided by the acquisition of Babe Ruth and other notable players, they played in their first World Series, and a major sports dynasty began. In 1927 they won 71 percent of their games, the highest percentage in the history of the Yankees. Between 1949 and 1964, the Yankees won the American League pennant fourteen times and the World Series nine times!

The Road to the 1960s for the Methodists

American Methodism did not start out as the largest Protestant denomination in the country. The historian William Warren Sweet captured the marginal status of Methodism in its beginning years in the United States. "Of all the religious bodies in America at the close of the American Revolution," he said, "the Methodists were the most insignificant," both in numbers and in influence.[1]

But as they did for the Yankees, things were to change for the Methodists. They grew dramatically, and by 1864, their status as the largest denomination in the country was reflected in the words of Abraham Lincoln. When a delegation of Methodists paid a visit to the president, he presented them with a letter saying, "While all churches are important, . . . it may fairly be said that the Methodist Episcopal Church . . . is, by its greater numbers, the most important of all."[2]

While the pace of Methodist growth slowed, the vigorous planting of new churches kept up with population growth. At the 1900 General Conference, the bishops of the church reported in their Episcopal Address that since the 1800 General Conference, the nation's population had grown by fourteen times while Methodist membership had grown by ninety-seven times.

Then Came the 1960s

The year 1964 came and went with the world as it had been. The Methodists had their General Conference in the spring and again ended the year with a gain in membership and the distinction of being the largest Protestant denomination in the country. Baby boomers began college in the fall just in time to watch the World Series between the New York Yankees and the St. Louis Cardinals. This year seemed like many years before and many years yet to come.

No one knew how significant 1964 was.

Beginning in 1965, the Yankees missed the World Series for eleven years, something unthinkable at the time. For the Methodists, 1965 was the last year of membership gain. Three years later The Methodist Church and The Evangelical United Brethren joined to form The United Methodist Church, but the new denomination continued to lose members at an even faster pace than the two denominations had separately.

The Dangers of Success

"It is one of the paradoxes of success," says Charles Handy, "that the things and ways which got you there are seldom those things that will keep you there."[3] Familiar patterns recur in unusually successful organizations. Things go well when there is congruence among mission, context, and structure, driven by the passion of people convinced that they are doing the most important thing in the world. But size and time take a toll. New people are removed from the original vision, and the structures needed for a growing and maturing organization create distance and layers that dampen passion. The momentum of past success continues, often for a long time, so long as the environment is relatively stable. It is when the context shifts that years of living off past success take their toll on an organization that long ago lost its capacity to adapt nimbly.

"Success tends to breed arrogance, complacency, and isolation," says Max De Pree. "Success can close a mind faster than prejudice. Success is fragile, like a butterfly. We usually crush the life out of it in our efforts to possess it."[4] One can see in the downturn of the mighty Yankees in the 1960s some of the same issues that faced other organizations, including The United Methodist Church, as the world changed around them.

- *Youth.* Their players were great, but stars such as Roger Maris, Whitey Ford, and Mickey Mantle were all in their thirties, not young by baseball standards.[5]

- *Diversity.* The Yankees were slow to add African American players, waiting eight years after Jackie Robinson broke the color barrier and after almost all the other teams had integrated.[6]

- *Changing context.* At the end of the 1964 season, major-league baseball moved to a draft for new players signing their first contracts, a change designed to limit the huge bonuses paid by the Yankees. Baseball fans were changing too. In 1964, the fledgling, hapless New York Mets drew a half million more fans than the pennant-winning Yankees.[7]

- *Leadership.* The innovative farm system built by the Yankees to develop talent was cut back to include only half the previous number of players. The assumption was that the best young players would want to play for the Yankees, with or without a farm system.[8]

When Good Practices Are No Longer Good Enough

A friend who is a dedicated layperson sent me a book a few years ago. It seemed a strange choice for a seminary president, as I was at the time. The book was a study of the disk drive industry. Although little of the book appeared to be applicable to the church, its central theme was intriguing.

The author, Clayton M. Christensen, wanted to discover why good companies do not stay atop their fields when confronted by certain types of change. He selected the disk drive industry for study for the same reason that those who investigate genetics study fruit flies. A generation for a fruit fly is one day, not thirty years. The disk drive industry has gone through generations at a "fruit fly" pace. Within a short time, there have been multiple generations of technology and multiple leaders in the industry.

Why is it, the author asks, that a company dominant in one generation of disk drive technology is virtually never the leader in the next generation? It is not poor management. Even as these companies lost their positions of market strength, their operations were exemplary. They listened to their customers, focusing on quality and responsiveness. Their leaders ranked among the best in the field.

What *did* happen? Christensen found that there is something about how decision making takes place in successful organizations that sows the seeds of eventual failure. While traditional management is well suited to what he calls "sustaining technologies" that continue to improve the product, such good management is inadequate when confronted with "disruptive technologies." The very practices that made an organization strong can become the practices keeping it from responding adequately to new challenges.

For example, the emergence of discount stores was a disruptive technology for department stores. What department stores did best was meet the needs of their primary constituents: upper-middle- to upper-class shoppers. But they knew little about the needs of a different constituency: lower-middle- to lower-class shoppers, now cultivated by a new breed of retailers.

So it was with the disk drive industry. While a dominant company sustained and perfected products for its customers, another company responded to changes in the environment by addressing different needs and constituencies. The new offering may not be as good as the original in a technical sense, but it more adequately addresses the needs of underserved constituencies. By the time more dominant companies discover that there are new groups with different needs, it can be too late.

Meaning for Churches

I sensed there was an application to churches and reviewed the cover letter my friend sent with the book. He wrote about the dominance of the Church of England, out of which Methodism emerged. Into that religious scene came disruptive technologies from the Wesleyan Revival, including field preaching, class meetings, and lay preachers. The response of the dominant religious group was to ignore or ridicule these practices, thinking they were neither particularly legitimate nor a threat to their own constituencies. By the time it became clear that these disruptive and different approaches were going to last, a new denomination was in place to stay.

My friend wrote then about the mainline denominations in the United States, the churches that were America's unofficial established church coming into the twentieth century. But things changed. He asked, "Could it be that these denominations are faced today with 'disruptive technologies' similar to those represented by Wesley's movement in England centuries ago? Could it be that we in the mainline churches are failing to see the efficacy of many of these disruptions, their lasting nature, and the new constituencies that they are reaching while we continue to operate as if nothing has changed?"

The most dangerous time for any organization is a time of success, when it does not understand the reasons for its success or the nature of its current vulnerabilities. As the church, we need to assess carefully and prayerfully our mission and our current effectiveness in achieving that mission. Thus we may save ourselves from doing what seems right based on our past instead of doing what actually furthers God's reign in our time.

Good practices cause congregations and denominations to take hold and minister faithfully. Those same practices may not be adequate for today. The test that John Wesley might use is: "Are the things you are doing bearing fruit?"

Attachment to Earthen Vessels

Consultant and author Gil Rendle reminds us, "Norms outlive the people who develop them."[9] Just as John Wesley knew that movements require organization and forms, he also knew that forms can outlast their power. He feared that Methodism may come to exist with the "form of religion but without the power."[10] In the United States, the quarterly conference was long the arena of revival and spiritual awakening for Methodists. Later, the camp meeting became the heart of a growing church's evangelistic enterprise, followed by the rise of the Sunday school movement. Each transition was difficult, especially for church leaders shaped by the languishing form. Upon hearing marvelous reports of persons reached for Christ through the Sunday school, conference leaders often implored Methodists to pay more attention to the loss of camp meetings.

Clinging to the forms of another time is not logical but completely understandable. Our identity becomes attached to the forms through which power came to us without our realizing that the form transmitted a power far greater than the earthen vessel that carried it. A form may no longer work for the new wine of new times, but our tendency is to expect leaders to preserve the old form and make it work. The need in such times is for leadership to guide God's people to discern the new thing God is doing and find the new expression of faith that permits the church to join God's redemptive work among God's people.

CHAPTER 1

A New Context

A prerequisite for leadership is an accurate understanding of reality; the first task for leaders is to help a group define its reality. Nehemiah helped define reality for his people when he said, "You see the trouble we are in, how Jerusalem lies in ruins with its gates burned" (Nehemiah 2:17). Any disagreement among hearers is not an occasion for argument but a further examination of the reality. The vision Nehemiah lifted of rebuilding the wall made absolutely no sense unless his description of reality was right. "Nothing is more limiting to a group," says Peter Senge, "than the inability to talk about the truth."[1] It is in interpreting "the signs of the times" (Matthew 16:3) that leaders help people face their most pressing challenges.

The next two chapters engage some of the new realities facing The United Methodist Church in the United States. New realities demand appropriate responses that fit the current circumstances and, at the same time, advance the mission.

Changing realities do not necessarily determine the future of The United Methodist Church, but neither can they be ignored. Giving attention to such changes does not come from a lack of faith in the future. In truth, this task is informed by the knowledge that the predecessor denominations to today's United

1

Methodist Church thrived best when they faced their own difficulties with both realism and faith. As in the past, a passionate combination of praying for miracles and working for results is the most viable way to participate in God's redemptive work while recognizing that finally it is God who brings the harvest.

This chapter makes the case for the necessity of a fundamental resetting of the financial baseline at all levels of the church. The purpose of the reset is partly caused by money but has to do with a lot more than money. The reason for the financial reset is to free our preoccupation from money to reaching people for Christ through vital congregations. The criteria that matter going forward must be built around reaching people, and the whole system needs alignment toward that goal.

The following chapter offers proposals for how this financial reset can happen. What follow then are chapters on how the church at the general, annual conference, and local church levels might focus attention to reach people for Christ during the coming years of relative strength. It is during these years that we have the greatest opportunity to respond faithfully and wisely to this critical calling—before we lose a large portion of current United Methodist members through death.

Money Up

The struggles of United Methodism today make it appear that there has been no success of any kind in a long time. Of course, this is not the case. As poorly as the denomination has done since the 1960s in virtually every category involving people, it has done well in other categories. Since the formation of The United Methodist Church in 1968, virtually everything related to money has increased dramatically—even factoring for inflation. These are such things as

- net assets,

- total giving and spending, and

- giving and spending per worshiper.

Increases	2009 as % of 1968
Net assets	217%
Total giving	144%
Giving per worshiper	178%
The 1968 figures are adjusted for inflation to 2009 dollars.	

In 1968, the net assets per congregation (values of property, buildings, and investments, minus debt) were about $105,000 per church (or $640,000 in 2009 dollars). By 2009, that figure had grown to $1.7 million per church. Eliminating investments from the calculations reveals that The United Methodist Church is a major holder of real estate. Based on 2009 property values, United Methodist property values reported by congregations were over $52 billion, including parsonages. And most of this property has no debt. In 2009, 81 percent, or 27,229 churches, reported no building debt.

Spending (and the giving required to fund the spending) continued to go up, even as fewer people participated. The total spending for all purposes in 1968 (using 2009 dollars) was $4,326,520,791, and $6,218,009,630 in 2009, for an increase of 44 percent after inflation.

Sometimes people view an increase in the average annual giving per year by worshipers as a sign of vitality. That may be the case, but it is not usually so when churches decline in attendance, as most United Methodist churches have in recent decades. Such increased per capita giving may reflect enhanced discipleship, but it may also reflect an aging and loyal membership giving more to meet increased spending. The average giving per worshiper grew from $1,083 in 1968 (in 2009 dollars) to $1,989 in 2009.[2]

People Down

While this remarkable increase in finances took place, virtually everything related to people went down, such as the number of churches, worship attendance, membership, professions of faith, and children and youth.

Decreases	2009 as % of 1968
Number of churches	80%
Worship attendance	78%
Membership	71%
Professions of faith	57%
Children and youth*	44%
*Children and youth figures begin with 1974 when they were reported for the first time.	

The remarkable, even shocking, contrast of these figures with those related to money serves as a reminder that money is a lagging indicator. When money becomes scarce, attention tends to focus on the reality that something is wrong. Yet it is obvious that something has been very wrong for quite some time that is only now manifesting itself as less money.

By observing these people-related declines, one can see a natural progression leading to today's financial situation. With fewer children and youth, there are fewer professions of faith, as the majority of new professions of faith come from those under eighteen. Fewer professions of faith mean fewer members. A smaller membership base leads to fewer worshipers. Fewer worshipers lead to fewer churches.

These figures of decline are not new revelations. But money can make up for, and tend to obscure, many failures. Life can go on much as it did before, as long as funding is in place. What is new today is the realization that the results of years of drawing down the United Methodist witness now have financial consequences. Aging members with increased assets and generosity cannot substitute forever for the neglect of the basics on which all giving depends—changed lives and transformed communities.

How Have We Made It This Far?

One might wonder how the denomination has sustained itself in the midst of such dramatic decline. How could fewer and fewer people give more money?

They did, until now. For thirty years, through 2007, United Methodist congregational giving, as a whole, which means all giving for all purposes by all congregations, increased from $100 million to over $300 million annually before factoring in inflation. That all stopped in 2008 when the gain was less than $5 million, as the national recession made its impact. Then in 2009, there was an absolute decline of almost $60 million.[3]

Some may be thinking, *Why can we not continue into the future as in the past once the recession is over? What is different now from the pre-recession years, when income increased so dramatically for so long? Surely we can expect the recession to end and more money to return.*

The practice of depending on fewer people to provide more money, which has been the economic operating model for The United Methodist Church from its beginning, is unsustainable in the face of demographic realities.

An Aging Membership

The aging membership of mainline denominations such as The United Methodist Church has been a continuing concern for many years, and for good reason. In the 1960s, when these denominations were growing, their membership was younger than the general U.S. population. But it seems clear that since at least the 1970s, the trend has been toward serving a membership older than the general population.

Since denominations do not track the ages of all their members, it is impossible to make an accurate comparison between the age of a denomination's membership and the age of the general population. There are, however, clues that indicate a denomination's membership may be getting older. Some representative samples and surveys demonstrate a general aging trend, in addition to experience and observations that give rise to the concern. People look around at many congregations and church gatherings and notice the stark absence of younger people.

The Lewis Center for Church Leadership of Wesley Theological Seminary monitors age trends in The United Methodist Church in the United States by examining one key indicator—death rates. At first, it may seem peculiar to focus on death rates. The death rates, while not exact indicators of age, do help show patterns that correspond generally to age. This is because 75 percent of deaths in recent years occurred among people aged sixty-five and older.[4]

A Lewis Center report found that while there are a few "pockets of youthfulness" among annual conferences in which the age of members appears to correspond with the region's general population, overall the denominational average age is much higher than the surrounding population. The report identified thirty-four annual conferences, representing 45 percent of denominational attendance, reporting death rates higher by 20 percent or more than those of their general population.[5]

The death rate among United Methodists in 2009 reflected a 35 percent increase over 1968, even though the death rate has leveled off in recent years, just as the national death rate has. These figures are reflected in the chart below showing the death rate (deaths per one thousand people) in the total U.S. population. It is clear from the chart that the national death rate is currently in a stable period. Government projections indicate that the current death rate plateau will continue until 2021.

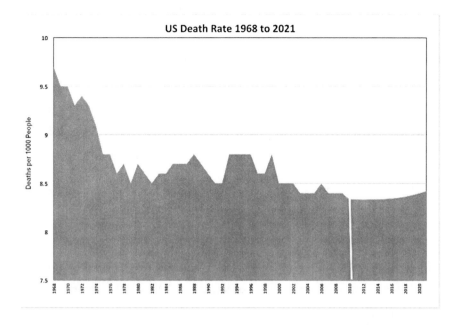

The Coming Death Tsunami

In the past several years, the world has witnessed the horror of two massive tsunamis, first in Indonesia and more recently in Japan. The loss of life and devastation surpass what most people can imagine. Those in other parts of the world are now learning about the fear with which our Asian neighbors have lived for centuries as they have experienced "minor" tsunamis and the terror that accompanies even small earthquakes and tsunami warnings.

In the Scriptures, prayers, and hymns of our tradition, our psalmists and poets described dire situations in the most compelling words they could find— a *flood* of mortal ills, as in the summer *drought*, a *famine* of compassion, life shaken as by an *earthquake*. Some images have become so familiar that we may no longer be moved by these stark words. Even so, one must be cautious when using analogies or metaphors that mirror such tragedies, recognizing that the effects of physical disaster differ from the results of the dire situations that writers attempt to describe.

So it is with the language of a *death tsunami*. What follows the plateau shown in the chart above can be called a *death tsunami*, for it has the potential to devastate the United Methodist witness in vast areas of the United States. This language is harsh and difficult to hear, as is the potential catastrophe challenging our church. It is predicted that between 2021 and 2050, there will be more deaths and a higher death rate than at any time since the 1940s. It is also predicted that there will 50 percent more deaths in 2050 than in 2010.

Death tsunami is too strong a term for the nation as a whole but not for The United Methodist Church. The vast majority of the projected deaths will be older non-Hispanic whites and African Americans, the two largest United Methodist racial groups in the United States. While the death rate shown on the chart goes up overall by 14 percent between 2010 and 2050, the increase for non-Hispanic whites is 26 percent.[6]

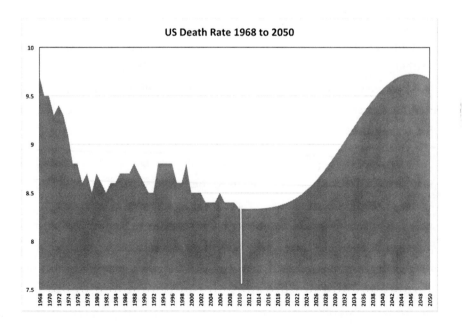

US Death Rate 1968 to 2050

The Dilemma

Comparing the situation facing The United Methodist Church to that of a congregation facing a similar dilemma may make it easier to appreciate. Countless churches have fewer worshipers today than they did ten or twenty years ago. Most of them, however, have budgets as large as or larger than they did when they had more constituents, even after adjusting for inflation. Such a congregation manages in the early years of decline by the greater giving of its fewer participants. As things get tighter, the lowering of expenditures combined with greater per capita giving maintains financial stability.

A church then gets to a point at which attendance has declined so much that making the budget each year becomes the preoccupation of the church and its leadership. Each year they search for that one new source of income or cut in spending so they can manage to make their plan. They also realize that even these yearly heroic efforts will not be enough going forward, as they note the high percentage of their annual giving that now comes from those over age seventy.

At some point along this journey, such a church has to make a basic decision. One option is to continue to live one year at a time and do whatever it takes to get by—even if necessary decisions harm long-term viability, and even knowing the church may, in the not-too-distant future, close.

But there is another option taken by some churches facing these circumstances. The second option is to acknowledge that things are not the same as in years past, and the previous financial baseline is no longer realistic. The church makes the difficult but ultimately lifesaving decision to reduce the financial baseline to one that is more realistic for the new circumstances. It is from this new and more appropriate baseline that the church can begin to build strength for the future. One reason that churches tend to do better after such a financial recalibration is that energy previously sapped through maintaining financial survival now can be spent for outreach and ministry.

A Window of Opportunity

Congregations with wise leaders recognize the emerging situation described above while there is time to reset their financial baseline and still have a critical mass of faithful members who can provide the foundation for a new, smaller, but more vital, chapter. Likewise, the financial reset needed by The United Methodist Church is not so urgent that inaction in the next few years will result in major disruptions. It is quite possible for the denomination to get by relatively smoothly for a time. Life can continue about as it has in the last ten years with adjustments around the edges to get through yet another year (fewer districts and conference staff, for example).

But a major denominational financial reset is required over the next five to ten years to position the church for seismic changes ahead due to the lack of alignment between the makeup of the denomination's membership (age and racial) and the realities of today's United States. As with any organization facing the future after forty-five years of unabated decline in its constituency, there must be a stepping back to a new and lower baseline in order to move forward. Otherwise, all energy goes, of necessity, to maintaining the old, unrealistic financial baseline.

The Operational Assessment Report (OAR)[7] of the Call to Action project is right in saying that the "creeping crisis" it identifies is not primarily financial and that opportunities are more related to identity issues such as "mission/values/culture."[8] But it is equally true that addressing structural and financial issues soon will provide the necessary space and energy to address the more substantive identity issues.

Doing everything possible to maintain giving at current levels or above will permit the church to survive in the short term, but not in the long term. The church faces two major challenges at the same time. One is reversing the drawing down of the United Methodist witness among the people of the United States. The other is the coming death tsunami. So our question is, What is required to survive the death tsunami and return to the growth of our witness at the same time?

Survival Is Not the Goal

To talk of survival does not mean that survival is an end in itself. The survival sought is not for an institution and certainly not for institutional forms or entities. However, The United Methodist Church represents a witness that has been preserved and reformed many times over generations. Those who talk casually about letting the church die so that something new emerges do not appreciate the interplay between continuity and change that characterizes renewal.

Church leadership is a response to God's love and action in the world revealed most clearly in Jesus Christ. Christian leadership is a channel of God's grace as it seeks the fulfillment of God's vision, and such leadership emerges out of the history, beliefs, and traditions of faith communities. While religious leadership always has a theological beginning, a theological grounding will not ensure either the discernment of or the fulfillment of God's vision. The task for each generation is to help the faithful discern an appropriate engagement to meet changed circumstances, new realities, and emerging needs. To do so, they must have an accurate assessment of those circumstances, realities, and needs. To the extent that leaders are able to accomplish these tasks, there are vitality and renewal within the religious tradition.

Faithful leadership understands the church not as an institution to serve and maintain but as an embodiment and instrument of God's aims revealed in Jesus Christ. The church indeed is to be Christ in the world, called to embody Christ's presence and participate in God's work of healing, reconciliation, redemption, and salvation in the world. Denominations become yet another of the earthen vessels in which the church seeks to carry the gospel. As with all such vessels, there is a temptation to focus on the container and not on the rich contents.[9]

The survival of any denomination or congregation is not a worthy goal. The continuation of a much renewed and changed manifestation of the Wesleyan witness of holiness of heart and life through The United Methodist Church is a worthy goal. We are the beneficiaries of this rich witness made possible through sacrifices most of us will never endure. To fail to give our best efforts to such revitalization would be tragic.

The death tsunami is coming. If it sweeps over a denomination already stretched to its limits in order to survive financially year by year, the result could be catastrophic.

However, if it comes to a church that has reset its baseline and demonstrated the ability to begin growing its witness through specific people categories, then the losses will occur, but will not deter the field of energy already moving in the denomination. Such movement will permit us to survive and to come out on the other side as a growing, missional, and spiritually alive instrument of God to spread holiness of heart and life across the land.

Thus resetting the financial baseline is not for the sake of survival. The resetting is to free the church and its leaders from the current preoccupation with all things financial in order to focus on the foundation of the United Methodist heritage in America that began with the goal of spreading scriptural holiness and reform of the nation.

The time to make choices is now—while there are still choices to make. Otherwise, circumstances will very likely make the choices for us in the future.

Gross, Not Net

David McAllister-Wilson, president of Wesley Theological Seminary, makes an important point in saying that in the coming years, churches should focus more on the "gross numbers" than the "net numbers." Usually this advice would make no sense. If a church receives twenty-five new members in a year while losing fifty members, it would generally be meaningless to focus on the gross gain of twenty-five rather than the net loss of twenty-five. But just as gross figures can be deceptive when viewed apart from the net, so also the net figures may be equally deceptive in the coming years.

Because of the coming death tsunami, it may be very difficult for churches to show net gains in a host of categories. Looking only to the net numbers will not only lead to discouragement but also may tell a false story of the spiritual energy of the congregation. Churches have relatively little control over losses, especially deaths. Churches have tremendous power to affect gains. So, even if the net figures for professions of faith minus deaths or new members minus lost members are negative for several years in a row, as long as the gross numbers for professions of faith and new members consistently increased during those years, there is reason to celebrate. The increasing gross numbers represent the church's spiritual vitality far better than the net figures. And it is precisely this positive energy that is needed for the years ahead.

CHAPTER 2

Resetting the Financial Baseline

Planning to live with less money is more than a strategy to adapt to the coming financial reality. It is a change of perspective. We continue to do everything possible to encourage giving, generously thank those giving, and report all the marvelous things God is doing with the giving. But we plan our staffing and ministries based on the money we can reasonably expect. Such a stance requires hard decisions. The trade-off, however, is enhanced freedom to focus on those things required to share God's love in Christ with more people, younger people, and more diverse people through vital congregations. Thus we can put an end to the continual drawing down of the United Methodist witness in the United States.

This resetting is not based on an assumption of scarcity. God's resources are boundless, and the financial resources of United Methodists, while not boundless, are far greater than current giving levels might indicate. No one argues that the present level of giving by United Methodists reflects fully committed discipleship. But giving is more than blind loyalty to denomination, conference, and local church budgets. While challenge and asking are important parts of giving, persistent patterns of relatively modest giving levels change only through spiritual growth. Therefore, we must reset in order to put our energy toward revitalization of the United Methodist witness.

Selecting only one locus for reductions will not accomplish a new baseline. These times require hard decisions at the denominational level as well as in annual conferences and congregations. We must plan to live with less money. Keeping spending within income will free us from the time, energy, and focus required to maintain income at unrealistic, higher levels. Just as cumbersome armor did not fit David in his struggle with Goliath, so a much smaller church increasingly finds the clothing of previous eras more of a burden than a blessing. Just as David found strength in what fit him, so the church today lightens its load, not to retreat, but to engage better the daunting challenges to God's reign in lives, communities, and the world. We reset not to survive but to grow toward that reign.

Reset: General Church

Resetting begins at the general church level. The General Conference, along with our agencies and institutions, must take the lead.

Address the cost of General Conference

Addressing the tremendous increases in the cost of General Conference is a step with powerful symbolic and financial impact. There are many factors associated with the increase, including the more global constituency of the delegations, but issues of cost go far beyond travel. The length and plethora of expectations involved in the current General Conference model make it increasingly complex and expensive. Simplistic solutions will not help. Addressing the size and length of the General Conference will save money but make the current model even more unworkable. Current responsibilities and procedures would fall on fewer people with less time at their disposal. A major rethinking of the purpose of General Conference in our day is needed and will be addressed when discussing refocusing at the general church level.

Review the role, size, and cost of general agencies and institutions

While the rise in numbers and influence of national denominational agencies, especially in the twentieth century, is not unique to United Methodism, we perhaps perfected the art. Russell Richey has documented the paramount place that agencies came to have in the shape and direction of the denomination. Mark Noll contrasts the heyday of this trend in the 1960s with times in the nineteenth century when some denominations might have no more than three or four staff members at the national level.[1] Neither extreme is the model for today. What happened as denominations grew and evolved fit what was happening with their traditions and was consistent with contemporary best practices of emerging and thriving organizations. The challenge today is to acknowledge we are in a different era with different needs and opportunities in order to make possible a new model with more missional traction.

The Call to Action Operational Assessment Report (OAR) found that the governing boards for general agencies are "generally too large and meet too infrequently" to fulfill their strategic, fiduciary, and generative responsibilities.[2] Although boards are smaller than they were previously, their very size still makes effective planning and decision making difficult. The OAR suggests boards of twelve to twenty-four members, much smaller than most, but not all, current boards. Such smaller boards can work if great care goes into their formation.

Smaller boards make meeting less expensive, but gathering people in one place for a meeting is perhaps the most overused and unproductive practice in the church at all levels. At the general level, its ineffectiveness is most expensive in terms of dollars, the time of participants, and the time taken from other responsibilities. This practice as the primary method of decision making cannot continue in a day with such rich technological options from which to choose. Just as in the case of the use of technology in education, some subjects lend themselves more easily to the use of distance technology. So with the work of the church, there will be tasks and responsibilities more conducive to the use of technology.

Shared services and the accompanying economies of scale recommended by the OAR[3] make sense and already happen in a number of cases, particularly around financial matters. More can be done. The downside can be greater distance and less "customer"-focused attention, though general board staffs with fewer personnel are finding such attention difficult to maintain at high levels. Where there are shared services, some entity needs to ensure accountability that the church's mission and values are maintained and not just that the services are provided efficiently.

The same hard thinking needs to go into a review of church institutions, including seminaries, where I have served much of my ministry. For example, there is no doubt that the establishment and care of a family of seminaries is one thing a denomination as a whole must do; no one else will. Other denominations will accept our students at their seminaries, but they will not establish and maintain United Methodist seminaries. Only The United Methodist Church will do this. Certainly the public will not provide seminaries as they do hospitals and schools. Yet even with a family of institutions so directly tied to the history and future of the denomination, hard questions have to be asked. One such question involves the best use of limited resources to accomplish the task of theological education shaped and molded by a United Methodist tradition, theology, and culture.

Link general church spending to accountability for outcomes, not activities

A traditional pattern of general church ministry is to provide funds to address a pressing issue, with responsibility assigned to an existing or new agency. The responsible party works hard and energetically to do things it discerns, along with others, will help address the issue. But it is unfair to provide funding without naming the specific outcome sought. The focus on outcomes is not so much to evaluate performance, at the end, but to shape how the initiative is planned. Without a description of the changed situation desired through the use of the funds, the focused action needed for change is not likely.[4]

Resetting means that general church funding emerges from the refocused role of the general church and goes to those things that the whole church looks to the general church to accomplish. The emphasis must move from *do* to *accomplish*. A mechanism of accountability is important but impossible without clearly defined goals. When a denomination decides to use a portion of the common wealth of the church, it must remember that every dollar is contributed to advance the mission of the church. Therefore, decisions to fund efforts require the church to name the outcome sought through such decisions.

Make pension decisions very carefully

The United Methodist pension program is one of the great success stories of the church. It is among the larger pension funds in the United States and is a reminder that the days of uncertain and inadequate pensions for clergy led to change for the better. While annual conferences are responsible for making some decisions and for funding pensions for their clergy, the denomination has one plan, thus the name of the general board uses the singular *pension*. Therefore, there is an inextricable relationship between general church and annual conference decisions. If an annual conference were to default on its obligations, the whole church shares responsibility for meeting the obligations.

The broad outline of any United Methodist pension plan should incorporate common best practices in society, though it is unlikely the church can exceed those practices. The General Board of Pension and Health Benefits can accomplish its mission only if realistic decisions are made. Clergy should expect an adequate pension, and the churches they serve should be confident that such a pension is in store for their pastors. By the same token, the clergy and churches should expect to contribute in a commonly accepted manner to ensure those pension payments are provided while the church's mission beyond clergy support advances.

If there were a time when clergy pension needs were neglected, that is no longer the case. When looking at financial resources devoted each year to pension support, one immediately sees the priority status of clergy pensions. Future decisions need to be made with great care. Any decisions that commit to long-term defined benefits need careful economic assumptions and must include projections of church trends. There are few places where overly optimistic economic assumptions combined with a reversal in the current United Methodist economic model (fewer people giving more money each year) could hurt the church more in terms of impact.

Reset: Annual Conference

The annual conference, as the basic body in the church, must reset in several ways. It must align its life and work with the changed context of the church. It must also create the policies and procedures that create necessary parameters in which congregations can reset.

Give congregations all responsibilities for clergy compensation and benefits

Independent churches understand that they must provide clergy salary and benefits. Having all such expenses paid directly by the congregation makes it far more likely that issues of sustainability, type of pastoral appointment, and adequate clergy workload are addressed. Having such "cost of doing business" benefits merged into an apportioned fund, as is done in some conferences, makes a church feel it is sending more money away for "the conference" than it is. At the same time, it shields everyone from facing up to local church sustainability issues that, if addressed creatively, can expand rather than diminish the church's witness.

Implementation may take place over a number of years so long as there is a fixed date for complete transition. If any congregations are to receive conference funds, then those funds should come from a mission fund available for use under two conditions: (1) the purpose of the grants is to extend the United Methodist witness within the bounds of the annual conference (not for congregational survival), and (2) there is a set time limit on such grants.

19

Review health benefits for both active and retired clergy to bring this benefit into alignment with commonly accepted practices of other employers

All clergy have a right of access to health care under provisions generally available to laity. However, the growth in cost of this benefit requires that it be reasonable but not beyond what would commonly be available outside the church.

The review needs to involve common employer/employee roles and responsibilities regarding heath care as well as coverage. For some conferences, this may mean that plans need to be upgraded and congregations will need to pay more. On the other hand, there may be some conference practices regarding how costs are divided between congregation and clergy, how retired health benefits are handled, and so on, that may need to be scaled back. In both cases, the transitions may occur over multiple years so long as a set time for full transition is in place. In addition, all conferences can benefit from the remarkable wellness efforts many conferences have connected with their health coverage. Ideally the church could exceed secular practices on a host of personnel benefits issues, but the only way that occurs now is by privileging one aspect of the church's mission over another, leaving fewer resources for everything else.

Convert assets to new church development

The growth in net assets of congregations in the last fifty years has been far above the inflation rate. Conferences need to find ways, consistent with their mission and the integrity of congregations, to establish policies to ensure that assets from closed congregations be used for new congregational development and not for other purposes, no matter how noble they may be. The tendency in a declining organization is to use such funds to shield itself against the effects of decline. In using these funds for new church development, careful metrics and accountability need to be in place so that funds coming from generations of faithful members will make possible many more generations of faithful ministry.

Instead of viewing very small congregations, such as those with fewer than ten in worship, in a passive way, conferences can have a proactive plan to assess ministry opportunities in these communities. Some will discover new ways of ministering. For others, the moment may have come to celebrate their history and close, thus becoming an Elijah Church that makes possible ministry for a new generation.

The goal of Elijah Church, a concept from the Virginia Conference, is not to close churches but to renew ministry. After the congregation assesses its current strengths and challenges with conference help, it explores several alternate scenarios for its future: (1) a renewed vision for revitalization, (2) relocation, (3) merger with another church and relocation to a new site, and (4) merger with another congregation using one of the current facilities.

Elijah Churches follow the biblical tradition of imparting a double share of their spirit in blessing a new ministry. Elijah Churches give up something to support new ministry for reaching new Christians. Options include (1) continuing while permitting a new ministry to begin in their building, (2) joining another church and giving the building to reach new populations, or (3) joining another church and investing the church assets in new churches.

Elijah Churches deserve special annual conference recognition. Just as many conferences include a "passing of the mantle" component in their retirement services, what if there were a time in which Elijah Church representatives passed the mantle to those in new churches, with both new church and Elijah Churches celebrated together?

Reduce annual conference size

A generation ago, annual conferences had 30 percent more members and could meet in a church. Some conferences today find it hard to locate a large enough meeting venue. While not in the power of an annual conference to change, the most important reform to deal with size, cost, participation, and age is to change the status of retired clergy. Retired clergy might choose to attend annual conference, but if they were not voting members and not included in the equalization-of-clergy-and-laity formula, the size of conference sessions would be reduced considerably. The exception would be those appointed to a local church in retirement. The pattern of including retired clergy came into being when there were few retired clergy. In earlier days most did not live long enough to retire. Some conferences today are approaching a time when there will be more retired elders than active elders, a reality that has no historical precedent. Consider the ratio of retired to active within ten years, given that now over half of active elders are between fifty-five and seventy-two years old, with the average elder retiring at age sixty-four.

Reduce the length of annual conference sessions

When the annual conference session and the annual pastors' school were the only times during the year when some clergy saw one another, meeting for about a week for each gathering made sense. In some conferences, families routinely attended such gatherings, often providing the closest thing the family had to a vacation. Today clergy and laity spend much of the year engaged with one another in connectional and other gatherings. Improved transportation, communication, and technology provide vastly different opportunities for connecting and sharing information regularly. Some conferences meet in shorter annual sessions than in the past, while others still need to rethink the cost in dollars and time for agendas often filled with things done as much out of habit as necessity.

Many things seen as inviolate annual conference traditions arose at some point in history, usually much more recently than we assume.[5] Some need to continue; others, not. All conferences evaluate their sessions, but few tackle major assumptions that make for long conference sessions. Asking simple questions of participants and acting decisively where there is significant consensus can within a few years achieve a far more focused—and shorter—annual conference session.

Review the impact on congregations of all financial obligations set beyond the local church before approving each year's conference budget

Conference leaders tend to think in terms of various levels of budget making and apportionments: general, annual conference, and sometimes jurisdictional and district. This is not how congregations experience financial claims by the church. For them, there is a major portion of their budgets over which they have little control except whether they will pay, which most work valiantly to do. From their perspective, the fact that the annual conference apportionments go up by 1 percent, for example, means little, since they experience conference apportionments as just one part of a larger basket of claims that include general, jurisdictional, conference, and district apportionments, plus health insurance, pension payments, and in some conferences, property insurance.

If an annual conference looks at budgeting for the coming year with all these items calculated for the impact on congregations, it is in a much better position to put together a budget that is viable for congregations. Seldom are all these variables on the table together, as they are when churches receive them. For example, in one conference that reduced districts, reductions in the conference budget occurred. However, within three years, the district apportionments had increased to surpass the conference savings. While district apportionments occur only in some conferences, the *Discipline* at least implies that, where they are used, they be set and presented for approval by the annual conference when the conference budget is presented.[6]

This task is not easy but is manageable if overseen by the Conference Council on Finance and Administration (CFA). A number of these items are not set by the CFA and usually never come before them. The General Conference sets general church apportionments; health insurance, pension decisions, property insurance, and district apportionments often are set in other arenas. However, if the annual conference is committed to vital congregations, it must take on this role of looking at the impact on congregations of all financial obligations set beyond the local church. This does not mean that decisions have to be made differently, but it should mean that at least one group in the connection is reminding everyone involved in setting any budgets that, in the end, those figures will make a difference in a congregation's ability to minister in the coming year.

Consider changing equitable salary policies and practices following a conference review

Equitable salary support can become another way to shield congregations from facing their sustainability issues. A policy of no minimum salaries and no equitable salary support would hasten the already fast-moving trend of using more part-time clergy to serve congregations. But in the end, if the number of churches able to support a full-time pastor is declining (as it is), there is not enough money available in any conference to support the current level of full-time clergy. This does not mean that conference mission funds cannot be spent to help congregations, but the same criteria mentioned above would be used: (1) the purpose of the grants is to extend the United Methodist witness within the bounds of the annual conference (not for congregational survival), and (2) there is a set time limit on such grants.

A few annual conferences have actually reduced their minimum salaries in recent years while others have left their rates unchanged. The common assumption is that lowering minimum salaries means pastors entering from seminary receive less income. This may happen in some cases, but it may well be that over the long term, especially if guaranteed appointments remain, the lower salaries will go to those clergy with a record of less than effective ministry and frequent moves.

Limit frequency of pastoral moves

One of the greatest claims on time and money in an itinerant system relates to the appointment process and pastoral changes. The United Methodist system that assumes a church for every pastor and a pastor for every church makes it difficult to limit the frequency of moves because mandatory moves (deaths and retirements, for example) have a domino effect on many clergy and churches. Numerous bishops believing in longer pastoral stays have found just how hard this goal is. However, if longer stays became the norm, even if some gaps in appointments occurred and interim pastors were used, the annual preoccupation around appointments (and the time and energy it generates) would arise for fewer churches and pastors. Also, the disruption and cost of the moves would be reduced. One other factor is that very few clergy are serving larger churches by growing their churches to higher attendance. Almost all serving large churches are getting there through moves. That trend does not need encouragement.

Implement targeted and restricted use of reserve funds

Conference reserve funds are necessary, but their purpose is compromised by uses not aligned with the mission of the annual conference. Two questionable uses of reserve funds are to supplement unpaid general church apportionments and to cover the same annual conference apportionment shortfalls year after year.

Every congregation should be encouraged to pay 100 percent of apportionments. However, the use of district or conference funds to supplement the congregations' apportionment payments skews their performance. At the same time it takes away funds that could be used for emergencies or other purposes not covered by apportionments. Some annual conferences have drawn from reserve funds to cover shortfalls in apportionments, only to deplete their reserves. While the goal of 100 percent apportionment payment is admirable, the privileging of any funds inevitably takes away from others and postpones facing up to the financial realities represented by underpayment.

In the case of annual conference apportionments, there is a stronger case for funding shortfalls because of unforeseen circumstances in any one year. However, to use reserve funds year after year for the same purposes that are not adequately supported delays acknowledging an unsustainable program. Each conference needs clear policies communicated well and broadly for how any reserve funds can and cannot be spent and for how long for any one purpose.

Gather clergy together for meetings less often

I have noticed two related trends recently in open-ended survey questions. One is a concern from laity about the amount of time their clergy are expected to spend away from their congregations. The other comes in studying how different generations of clergy perceive things. Baby boomers tend to think Gen Y clergy are too obsessed by technology, while Gen Y clergy see boomers as compulsive about always getting together for meetings. These same young clergy are not against communicating; they are in virtual constant communication with vast networks of colleagues and friends about a host of matters.

Calculate the days in a year available to a pastor and then subtract days off, vacation, holidays, annual conference, pastors' school, orders' meetings, required training, district meetings, and conference and district responsibilities. It is easy to see why there is a concern from laity and clergy about the time away from the congregation. Failure to think through such gatherings in a careful way—and from the perspective of those attending the meeting and not those calling the meeting—may be one reason for Gil Rendle's observation that "denominations routinely want more of a connection with congregations and clergy than congregations and clergy want with their denomination."[7]

Denominational leaders will do well to remember Francis Asbury's attitude about clergy priorities. After clergy visitors showed up when Asbury preached in a local setting, he wrote of their presence: "We are pleased to see them; but would be better pleased to know they were on their circuits, faithfully at work."[8]

Reset: Congregation

To reset the financial baseline in congregations, laity and clergy must first assess what is the current status of the local church. They must name their reality.

Examine the congregation's financial history for the last five years

When examining the most recent local church annual budgets compared with actual income, what patterns emerge? Churches commonly receive less money than what their budgets project. However, churches need to pay attention to the gap, if there is one, to see whether it gets greater each year. How much impact did any budget shortfall cause? Modest shortfalls normally make no differences, while larger shortfalls result in reduction in staff, programs, or payment of apportionments.

Examine the effort required to meet each year's budget

Congregational financial health requires careful attention and work in the best of circumstances. Here the goal is to see whether there is any change taking place in the proportion of time and energy required to meet the budget each year. Are inordinate effort and attention required to meet the budget?

Has attendance gone down as the budget continues to rise?

If this is the case, it means fewer people give more money each year. That is precisely the denominational pattern that is now beginning to break down.

How much of the giving in each of the past three years came from persons age seventy or older?

This percentage could be called a church's "vulnerability index." A portion of increased giving in churches in recent decades has come from an increasing number of members who are both older and loyal in the use of resources they accumulated over a lifetime. Most of them did not start out giving at such levels. They came to their current level of giving usually through a combination of growth in discipleship and increased financial resources. Generous givers of the future probably will follow the same route. Therefore, to neglect reaching new people and teaching stewardship because the church already meets its budget through the generosity of a few is shortsighted ministry.

Examine practices and policies for any endowment or other permanent funds

Some churches have funds for which an invested principal makes possible funds for ministries through earnings. Here are some questions for such churches:

Is the money invested to maintain its value? If the investment goals and performance do not provide for returning to the principal at the rate of inflation, then the value of the funds decreases in buying power every year.

Do we have an appropriate spending rate? Many churches spend what is "earned" each year. This is a certain way to erode the value of the endowment. Another way is to separate spending from annual earnings. A church may have an investment goal of achieving over any multiyear period (seven to ten years) an average annual rate of total return of inflation plus the "spending rate" established by the church. For example, if the church assumes inflation at 2 percent and desires to spend 4 percent for various ministries each year, then the church needs an investment plan to achieve an average annual total return (interest, dividends, and appreciation) of 6 percent. This preserves the value of the original gift and gives a conservative, yet stable, source of income year by year.

Is the principal protected? Most endowed funds have policies or bylaws that severely limit the ability of the church to draw from the principal except in the most extreme circumstances and following detailed steps. Increasingly, despite such requirements, churches are drawing from permanent funds for current needs.

Examine debt

Has the percentage of annual expenditures going to principal and interest on debt increased in recent years? Does the congregation anticipate more debt?

Is the debt compromising the ability to expand ministry rather than facilitate such ministry?

Examine deferred maintenance

One common way for congregations to balance budgets in difficult times is through the accumulation of deferred maintenance. Each congregation must consider whether this is the case. Is there a systematic plan to fund at least a minimal level of ongoing capital renewal and replacement needs of the church facilities in addition to routine cleaning and maintenance?

Consider whether all assumptions about financial implications are sustainable

For some churches, long-held assumptions may need questioning if year after year short-term solutions do not address the financial dilemma. These are hard considerations. Some may be in a historic and much-loved building they no longer can maintain. Others may face the prospect of a less than full-time pastor. Another church may need to explore merger. These big decisions come only after many other options prove impossible.

The OAR names the need for The United Methodist Church to develop "alternative approaches to creating affordable places of worship that meet the Church's mission objectives." These models "would explore various clergy and lay staffing structures and different real estate models for geographic locations with varying membership/attendance sizes and trends." The goal of such an effort is to develop places for new and existing places of worship that better "match membership/attendance levels with cost structure in a mission compatible fashion."[9]

Reset: Everywhere

Resetting the financial baseline must happen at every level of the church. It must also occur everywhere—not only in large boards and small churches, not only among young clergy and retired bishops. If this movement is going to position The United Methodist Church for the future, there must be shared imagination and creativity and shared sacrifice.

Each person and group, given its particular calling, will have a different role. But all must have a common vision that keeps everyone focused on the new thing God is calling us to be and do. Otherwise, the danger is that some will see their interests as privileged and not subject to resetting, with tragic divisions occurring among us.

Resetting can bring hope to every corner of The United Methodist Church. Everyone everywhere is crucial to its success.

CHAPTER 3

General Church

The United Methodist Church is facing a "creeping crisis of relevancy," according to the Call to Action Operational Assessment Report.[1] The report identifies internal signs of challenge related to relevancy, such as lack of mission clarity and congruency. To achieve clarity of identity and purpose and the essential corresponding coherence throughout the entire denomination, the role and functions of the General Conference and the general church will need to be far more narrow, focused, and effective. To achieve this goal, The United Methodist Church will need general church leadership that is

- identity-shaped,

- mission-driven,

- values-bounded, and

- context-appropriate.

Focus: Identity-shaped

The beginning point for all renewal is theology and tradition. If church leaders are to discern the "new thing" God is doing, it is well to "look to the rock from which we were hewn and the quarry from which we were dug," to use images from Isaiah. John Wesley led an emerging movement that used new practices yet always stayed grounded in an identity of rich and historic faith and tradition. Renewal came through the Wesleyan movement not by abandoning heritage but by rediscovering and reshaping tradition for a new context.

A strong theological and historical identity can withstand a host of organizational mistakes, but even the most careful management cannot overcome a lack of shared identity. The early forerunners of United Methodists in the United States were small in number and lacked resources; yet they had such a strong internal identity and culture that miraculous things happened. To endure, any movement needs a powerful and commonly shared integrating identity.

As time goes by and especially when difficulties arise, an organization with a loss of shared identity turns blame inward, aimed at a host of perceived foes. More narrow identities replace the larger shared identity as rallying points for various constituencies. Since none of the smaller identities have the movement's common good at their core, there is no unifying center. Thus, in a shared leadership system such as United Methodism, the power of the "invisible leader" of common identity and purpose goes missing.

Rather than inhibit diversity, a shared core identity makes greater diversity possible. Commitment to the center allows multiple expressions based on the common core; but without a unifying center, mere inclusion becomes only a gathering of unrelated differences. Wesleyan inclusion—of both ideas and people—requires a common foundation. From this common foundation and shared identity come unity of purpose, direction, and commitment, but never uniformity. As Gil Rendle contends, the increasing diversity of the church makes uniformity and conformity impossible but requires a "shared center."[2]

Diversity and inclusiveness flower not as ends in themselves but as by-products of a faith that unites people more tightly than differences can separate.[3] Shared identity permits a loosening of the tight reins of central control to permit what Rendle describes as a "disparate group of forms of congregations."

These emerge in a denomination "less about regulations and uniformity and more about a shared story of purpose and identity that holds a network of unmatched congregations, leaders, and people in a whole."[4]

All the theological streams inspired and fed by the Wesleyan spirit continue to make important contributions to a more faithful Christian witness today and need inclusion in United Methodism's theological identity. The goal is not to outdo those with whom we disagree. The goal is to turn with them toward the larger needs of a hurting world, even as we continue to help one another grow in our understanding of the mystery and richness of God's revelation.

While theology is the beginning point of shared identity, the Wesleyan movement began not as a doctrinal debate but as a renewal movement. Wesley's conferences gave much time to the discussion of theology, and portraits of Wesley as a leader of a revival with little interest in doctrine miss the mark.[5] Doctrine, however, served not so much as a creed demanding consent as it did a channel through which the love of God was introduced to people, making possible a saving encounter with Jesus Christ. Theology served the mission— growth in the love and knowledge of God and social witness.

Focus: Mission-driven

Referring to Russell Richey's work on connectionalism, Bishop Grant Hagiya notes that "mission was fundamental to American Methodism—an almost ontological state of being, deeply ingrained in our structure and identity." He goes on to note that with growth and complexity, mission became a function among others, and thus "the original consciousness of mission as core identity faded more and more."[6]

The apparent lack of alignment of mission and behavior observed by the Call to Action researchers may be behind much of the church's dilemma. United Methodists surveyed often reported seeing no connection between the work of many denominational bodies and the stated mission of the denomination of "making disciples of Jesus Christ for the transformation of the world."

The survey results remind me of a congregation that spends months of study, debate, and deliberation on a new mission statement. Once in place, the new mission appears prominently on the church website, on the front of church bulletins, and framed and put in strategic locations around the church facilities. However, the way things operate in worship, Sunday school, trustees, and finance does not change. A few years later a church survey finds little connection between the mission and the church's ministries, and its leaders are surprised.

In both examples, people do not see connections because there are not many. Various entities do not see their roles through the lens of the mission but view the mission through the lens of their responsibilities. In reality, the groups may have been established originally to advance the mission of the time but long ago became responsible to "do their jobs"—important tasks, but not necessarily driven by the mission.

Focus: Values-bounded

In the early years of any organization, mission is paramount, and values are assumed. Values are commitments honored in fulfilling the mission. They are as important as the mission but never viewed apart from the mission. Values do not compete with mission, but shape how the mission is fulfilled. After an organization has been around for a long time, and particularly when it is in decline, values tend to supplant mission in importance. Thus a time of decline grows worse, since nothing contributes more to weakness than forgetting purpose. The problem with making values the priority is that one can fulfill values perfectly while being unfaithful to the mission.

In times of decline, people are fearful that the values that mean most to them will get lost, so they contend against people pushing other values, and in the process everyone forgets the priority of the mission. It is as if people are arguing so much over which stanza of the hymn to sing that everyone forgets the tune. In such cases, values trump mission in decision making. Both mission and values are nonnegotiable, but their sequence is crucial. Mission comes first, and values represent those commitments within which we fulfill the mission. The United Methodist Church is blessed with a richness of values: biblical, evangelical, ecumenical, inclusive, diverse, justice, spirituality, peace, and education, to name but a few. Losing sight of such values leads to weakness, just as viewing values apart from mission leads to weakness.

Focus: Context-appropriate

In seminary I learned from James F. White three criteria for making decisions regarding appropriate worship practices: historical, theological, and pastoral. No one of the three is sufficient as a guide. One may be able to justify a practice on historical and theological grounds that would not be pastorally appropriate for a particular congregation. The practice may actually get in the way of meeting spiritual needs. In denominational life, the word *context* serves a purpose similar to White's use of *pastoral*.

All actions throughout denominational life must be identity-shaped, mission-driven, and values-bounded. They must also be context-appropriate. Different contexts require a degree of flexibility and nimbleness to manifest identity, mission, and values in ways appropriate to those contexts.

In the early decades, when Methodism spread in England and North America, as David Hempton has noted, it "changed and adapted to new contexts, but it remained recognizably Methodist, not just evangelical, wherever it became established." He goes on to use a biological metaphor of Methodism as "a recognizable religious species" that "grew, adapted, and procreated according to the suitability of its environmental conditions."[7] In the United States, adaptability came easily for the early preachers because their context was the only world they knew. "They were natives in the early republican world of egalitarianism, geographic mobility, and the religious free market," notes John Wigger, "a world in which the older denominations were still but immigrants."[8]

Notice how Hempton uses the word *recognizable* to describe the early Methodists. The Methodists expressed their faith in ways appropriate for their context, but they always knew they were different from the larger society. In the history of the United States, Methodists have moved from subculture to counterculture to virtual identification with the predominant culture.[9] This cultural identification that erases the counter-status-quo nature of the gospel is always a danger. There is inevitable tension between adapting to one's context and becoming captive to it.

The fear of cultural captivity is not an excuse to avoid engaging a changing culture. While United Methodism is now more on the sidelines of U.S. culture than in the past, it is by no means a marginal religious sect. But we know that no living things continue to thrive generation by generation without environmental adaptability.

What Might This Mean?

Role of General Conference

Mainline denominations have often been fundamentalists of structure rather than of doctrine. It is not working today. The regulatory tendencies of mainline denominations seem to increase as their traditions shrink. The OAR finds such "management through legislation" leading to "an increasingly rigid and rule bound culture" precisely at a time the church is attempting to adapt to a radically changed environment. The 2008 *Discipline* uses the term *shall* 4,863 times in naming mandates while using the term *may,* giving guidance with flexibility, only 1,382 times.

It is time to rethink the role of General Conference into a more modest, yet essential, role. It is time to move from structures of control to a culture of trust and grace. The General Conference could become the primary arena for defining three of the four general church dimensions:

1. identity-shaped

2. mission-driven

3. values-bounded

What if the General Conference came together to address matters of doctrine and United Methodist self-understanding and then gave greater freedom, such as central conferences have today, in matters of structure and regulations? Thus General Conference would be a time for celebration, worship, and engagement with those elements of United Methodist identity that unite across all boundaries and differences. The General Conference would deal with identity, mission, and values while leaving it to global regional conferences to establish those policies and procedures they need to carry out their context-appropriate ministry.

We live in a time when people are not anxious to have others make decisions for them or to speak for them. A more humble General Conference could recognize that less is more, in both control and pronouncements. In the more diverse and global church of today, achieving a majority vote for a change or statement means little unless there is a much larger consensus within the church on the matter.

Role of continental conferences

Thus far, there is no such thing as a continental conference, but such will be essential if we are to have context-appropriate leadership. The commitment to a global church is universal within the denomination. The growth of United Methodism in the central conferences of Africa, Congo, West Africa, and the Philippines is thrilling to behold and reminds U.S. members of our own earlier chapters.

Frequently, conversations about the global church begin with claims that the denomination is too "U.S.-centric." Surely that is the case given its history. But there is a sense in which the United Methodist Church *should be* U.S.-centric, in the same way it needs to be Africa-centric or Asia-centric. To think that we can effectively take structures designed primarily for one nation and extend them into global entities likely means that no group gets what it needs. Therefore, a more modest role of General Conference in the future can make possible far greater decision making for continental conferences. It would reflect what we have now in the central conferences, which are able to modify portions of the *Discipline* to fit their circumstances. This very provision shows how the current system of one body making decisions for a global church is unworkable.[10]

Role of episcopacy

A discussion of episcopal leadership presents a dilemma for some, but such a conversation is critical to the future of The United Methodist Church. Many are suspicious of episcopal leadership, perhaps because of the fear of abuse of authority. People are correct to be wary of authority when it takes the form of power over others. However, there is an authority essential to the effective fulfillment of one's calling to ministry, including the calling of the episcopacy. Without understanding and claiming this authority, bishops will be reticent to exercise their leadership and, thereby, be unfaithful to their calling and to our church.

Authority of calling

Authority has to do with responsibility, not privilege. Christian authority is not about status in relationship to others but about what God's will is for each of us and how faithful we are in fulfilling God's call. Christian leadership responds to the authority of calling in contrast to the power of position, and the bishops' focus must be on their relationship to God's vision for the church they serve. In this light, episcopal leadership gains its power not from office but from its faithful alignment with the larger call of God's purpose.

From the beginning, the church called persons to various roles of leadership on behalf of the whole church. These roles are not private possessions to guard and protect. Leadership is about service, not prerogative. We all need authority in different ways based on the unique callings that God, the church, and our context place on us. Proper authority is essential to carry out God's vision for the church and the world.

Virtually any study of United Methodism points out the difficulty of change because "no one is in charge." That is not by accident. One person interviewed in the Call to Action project said the church "has a systemic allergy to authority."[11] There has been a strong distrust in American Methodism about having too much power in one place, making it impossible for anyone to serve as "wagon master."[12] Such a system works much better in good times than in bad.

Alignment and accountability

Perhaps the greatest roles for episcopal leadership are alignment and accountability. Oversight of identity, mission, and values rightly belongs to episcopal leadership. They cannot do it by themselves, but small groups of bishops, joined by equally modest numbers of clergy and laity, could guide the alignment of general church life with the mission of the denomination. The Council of Bishops is an appropriate arena for accountability, so long as they submit to accountability for their stewardship of the church's identity, mission, and values.

To serve these new roles, the church needs to expect less of bishops in some other areas, and bishops need to discipline themselves to permit time for their general oversight of the church. Specific changes to enhance episcopal leadership include the following:

1. General oversight of the Church's mission

The Constitution of The United Methodist Church gives the Council of Bishops "general oversight and promotion of the temporal and spiritual interests of the entire Church." But as Russell Richey and Tom Frank note, this power is shared with the General Conference, which has "full legislative power over all matters distinctively connectional," including setting the powers and duties of the episcopacy.[13] These two constitutional principles are eminently compatible if one assumes that all entities of the church are accountable to the whole as represented by the General Conference.

Why turn to the bishops for this unifying oversight? The bishops have a perspective unlike that of any other leaders of the church. It is a perspective informed by the diverse parts of the church with whom they interact regularly and also by their work with colleague bishops. Bishops usually rise to the expectation that they will bring their distinctive experience and also grow as leaders who now must represent more than a personal agenda.

While bishops are "general superintendents," the reality is that bishops can have far more influence within their episcopal areas than they have anywhere else. In that sense, bishops function in a more diocesan model than the early general superintendents. The area-specific reality is not going to change and probably should not. Any time away from their episcopal areas must be substantive and must include enough leverage to ensure the church is doing what it says through the General Conference and continental conferences, that is, to carry out their general oversight of the church.

The church desperately needs the general oversight and accountability roles of the Council of Bishops. The direction of the oversight comes from the General Conference itself. One thing that makes such oversight difficult is that currently the Council of Bishops is one of dozens of groups that share oversight, resulting in the substance of their oversight being what Richey and Frank call "unstructured and indeterminate." They cannot give the oversight the constitution requires because current legislation makes them one alongside many, with no group able to ensure the alignment and accountability so needed.

Oversight and accountability through the Council of Bishops could occur with the smaller general boards called for by the OAR, with a modest number of bishops along with clergy and laity selected because of the gifts they bring to the particular board's work. Bishops currently serve as individual members of general boards. But the new model suggested here is different in that the bishops now would see their role on behalf of the General Conference and the

Council of Bishops. The Council is responsible to make sure the priorities and actions taken by each board flow from General Conference–approved identity, mission, and values.

At the same time, this oversight is corporate in that the bishops also serve on behalf of the Council. The Council in its work as a whole can clarify the strengths and weaknesses that need attention by the bishops assigned to the boards. The bishops are not representing themselves but the Council, whose responsibility is to the General Conference.[14] Should the Council misuse this oversight power, the General Conference is fully capable of addressing the matter within four years.

2. Creation of a four-year set-aside president of the Council of Bishops

Rejected in the past, this proposal causes some to fear too much centralization. To the extent that centralization permits greater focus, such movement may be valuable. The greater fear is that such a new position is sabotaged by turning it into a ceremonial and ecumenical representative role. What is called for is an effective leader *for* the denomination rather than *on behalf of* the denomination. Recent presidents of the Council of Bishops provide better models for this new role than heads of other denominations. Despite the constraints of both role and time, these episcopal leaders exercised tremendous leadership by force of their ideas, credibility, perseverance, and willingness to engage all their colleagues and others.

3. Assumed length of assignment to an area to be twelve years

Leadership takes time. If the bishops and the conferences know going in that the expectation is for a lengthy relationship, the chances of success become greater. If the assumed length of episcopal service in an area were to be four years, then the office of bishop becomes increasingly ceremonial and honorific. If the assumed tenure in one area were to be eight years, then the office takes on a more managerial shape. The bishop is there long enough to make changes and improvements, though probably not long enough to guide more systemic and cultural changes. If the assumed tenure is twelve years, it is much more likely that long-lasting adaptive leadership occurs.

With the revision of responsibilities for the General Conference, the role of the annual conference becomes even more crucial. It is to this basic unit of the church that we turn next.

CHAPTER 4

Annual Conference

The Constitution of The United Methodist Church identifies the annual conference as "the basic body in the Church."[1] The annual conference admits persons into ordained ministry, and it is from the annual conference that clergy go to their assignments. Clergy hold their membership in the annual conference and not in congregations. This gives United Methodism what Russell Richey describes as a "missional ecclesiology" from which flow "Methodism's distinctive itinerant and appointive commitments."[2]

Identity as Basic Unit

With the focus on local churches in recent times, it may seem strange to many to find such a prominent role for what they view as a middle structure between denomination and congregation. The annual conference, however, will continue to have a pivotal role in the mission of United Methodism, and because of new circumstances, it will exist in different ways in the future than in the past. The centrality of the annual conference cannot remain unless historical and theological values are applied to fit changing times, even as John Wesley felt free to modify tradition for the sake of the gospel. As long as bishops appoint clergy, the connection of the pastors to the annual conference is a given. Congregations and laity likely will be more guarded in their relationship to the conference.

The "sent ministry" reflected in the ecclesiology represented by the annual conference is vitally important. From a missional perspective, however, there is another sense in which the annual conference is the basic unit in a way that no other unit of the church is. Even with the mergers that have increased the geographic size of conferences, the annual conference continues to be the arena in which the culture and ethos of a region are best known and appreciated. It is appreciated not in the sense of thinking that everything is good, but in understanding how it came to be and how to relate to it in caring and logical ways. This does not mean that the territory encompassed by an annual conference, even the smallest, is monolithic. The opposite is usually the case. But it is within the annual conference that subtleties and variations are best understood.

Usually persons outside the annual conference think of states or regions represented by annual conferences in a monolithic light. I was a pastor in Mississippi for many years. For many outside Mississippi, the state has a singular identity. While there are some common characteristics, there are stark differences between churches on the Gulf Coast and those in the Delta. Virginia may bring to mind certain images for the outsider, but within the conference, participants understand that the D.C. suburbs of northern Virginia, Shenandoah, Tidewater, and Richmond are in some ways as different as different states.

I have been struck over the years by how intimately acquainted conference leaders tend to be with the various cultures and people in their midst. They show a remarkable ability to operate with both integrity and understanding among the differences within their conferences. At the very least, at the annual conference level there is a heightened sense of how important it is to account for the varieties of cultural and religious expression.

This awareness means that the annual conference is the level at which propagation of the Wesleyan witness through The United Methodist Church is best guided. In the new context in which the church lives, that role is critical.

Current Purposes for the Annual Conference

"The purpose of the annual conference," as stated in the *Discipline*, "is to make disciples of Jesus Christ for the transformation of the world by equipping its local churches for ministry and by providing a connection for ministry beyond the local church; all to the glory of God."[3] The stated mission begins with the clear denominational mission of making disciples for the transformation of the world. The direction is outward and missional. Largely, however, the dimensions of "equipping" and "connecting" that follow have led congregations to look to the annual conference for what it can do "for us."

Similarly, an unfortunate direction for both conference leaders and clergy is to see the annual conference as an employment association for clergy. Increasing attention is given in many conferences to finding places for the clergy. With that beginning point, the needs of the same congregations that the conference seeks to equip for mission may be undermined by the mandate to place clergy. If congregations and clergy are asking only what the conference is doing for them, it is hard to imagine that the annual conference can remain central to the life of the church. Our history and theology are better than that. We at our best are better than that. Our rich heritage deserves far better.

The "Calling" of the Annual Conference

In thinking about the appropriate roles for any entity in the church, one must consider the "calling" of this unit. What does the entire church look to this body to do, so that if it does not do it, no one else can or in all likelihood will? This thinking gets away from power and prerogative and turns thinking toward what the whole church has a right to expect. What should faithfulness and fruitfulness look like for this part of the church?

The focused work of the annual conference needs to flow from the denominational mission, address the special calling of the annual conference, and have all roles flowing from and shaped by that calling. What are those things that no other body has the mandate (calling) or the ability to do and thus belong to the annual conference?

Focus: Steward and extend the United Methodist witness

The calling of an annual conference is different from that of a congregation. A distinctive task of an annual conference—which no other unit of the church has—is to steward and extend the United Methodist witness within the geographical bounds of the conference.

Focus is a particular challenge for an annual conference where attention is spread thinly over a myriad of good interests, each with its own protective constituency. In trying to do things for an array of constituents, it fails to do what only the annual conference can do. And because of this, every annual conference in the United States, even those few that are growing, is drawing down its presence within its borders as the United Methodist percentage of the population decreases. If the beginning point for contemporary United Methodist witness is to be consistent with our early American history, that is, starting with the people—all the people God has given us—then this failure either to preserve or to extend the United Methodist witness is a betrayal of our tradition and calling.

Enhancing and extending the United Methodist witness take seriously that this witness has many forms. It represents presence in congregations and worshipers and also in ministries, partnerships, and public impact. To capture the wholeness of the Wesleyan witness, essential elements will include knowing God; proclaiming Christ; serving others, especially the poor; and seeking justice.[4] Worship and discipleship are the foundation for all ministries, as with earlier examples of vital Wesleyan witness. It is not likely that even the finest ministries will survive and expand if the church's efforts to connect people with the love of God in Jesus Christ expressed through worship, study, and service continue to decline.

Enhancing and extending the United Methodist witness within the bounds of the conference, if not done by the annual conference, will not be done by anyone else. This should be a concern not only for conference leaders but also for all clergy and lay members of the annual conference. When clergy and laity come together for annual conference, some may see their roles as looking out for the interests of their congregations. Not so. That is an appropriate role within the congregation but not within the annual conference. At the annual conference session, clergy and laity are not representatives of congregations but stewards of the mission of the annual conference. Decisions must be made in light of their impact on whether they will enhance and extend the United Methodist witness among the people within the borders of the conference. If they are not looking after that mission, no one else in the church will.

The annual conference is a powerful symbol of the connectional principle; that is, the church is not complete in any one manifestation but is part of God's work in a larger connection. Without a steward mind-set, vast opportunities to advance God's work are neglected. The populations different from those that make up existing churches have no voice. Those younger than the constituency of annual conference sessions may be forgotten. Places where there is no United Methodist witness or no effective witness, given the potential, will have no spokespeople.

This tension surfaces when the need for new congregations comes up against the perceived interests of existing churches. Or the needs of large membership churches are seen in competition with those of small membership churches. The focus, instead, must be on how best to enhance and extend the United Methodist witness, which will require new and existing churches as well as large and small churches. Small churches, for example, must be deeply concerned with what large churches need to be strong because the ability to enhance and extend the United Methodist witness rests heavily on large churches. Furthermore, small churches understand in their best moments that an annual conference requires a healthy mix of small, midsize, and large churches to function. Small churches know better than any other group that without the large churches, the small churches alone could not carry the mission of the conference. In the same way, large churches must be watchful that small churches have what they need to fulfill their callings because they know that they cannot do the ministry now done by the small churches. Each has a stake in the success of others. But without a common destination—a stronger United Methodist witness—the gravitational pull will always be to lesser goals.

Focus: Leadership requisite to accomplish the mission

Ordained ministry

Integral to the understanding of ordained ministry in The United Methodist Church is the annual conference's role in examining and approving those seeking ordination. Individuals discerning a call to ministry must follow a process designed to assure that they are genuinely called and sincerely faithful, that they are educationally and psychologically prepared for the rigors of ministry, and that they are fruitful and effective in service.

Over many years, the church has increasingly asked more of people seeking ordination. Such changes also affect boards of ordained ministry. There is a sense in which the church is asking boards to solve problems not of their making. For example, the impact of continuing membership loss and concern for ineffective clergy puts more pressure on those who screen new clergy. There is a misguided hope that examining new clergy longer and more closely will compensate for problems caused by some current clergy.

Guaranteed appointments

One major factor putting pressure on the ordination process is the guaranteed appointment for elders. The ordination process carries much weight since it must function as an insurance policy, ensuring that those ordained have the capacity to continue in guaranteed appointments. Without guaranteed appointments, the pressure put on board members would dramatically drop. As a veteran of several terms on boards of ordained ministry, I can testify that there is a subtle but powerful difference in anxiety about wrong decisions regarding elders and deacons. Boards know that if deacons, not covered by guaranteed appointments, fail to keep up in their training, are unable to work with people, and do not demonstrate effectiveness, there will be no place for them to serve since they must find their own employment.

Guaranteed appointments were put in place originally to avoid the discriminatory use of appointive power by bishops. There are now other ways to address the possibility of such action without granting a blanket right to all clergy. The tide of history is moving away from elites guarding their prerogatives while the mission of their organizations struggles. Especially in a denomination that increasingly looks to local pastors, lay ministers, deacons, and lay staff for congregational leadership, it will be difficult for a shrinking cohort of elders to make an exclusive claim for guaranteed employment. Ending guaranteed appointments may cause anxiety, but there is already anxiety in the system as fewer and fewer pastoral charges are able to pay what annual conferences require for elder compensation. This is one pressure moving annual conferences more into the role of employment societies for clergy. It is hard to see how the current trajectory can be interrupted without change in the guaranteed appointment and equitable salary concepts.

The guaranteed appointment debate often refers to a "covenant," though congregations have never felt a part of this covenant in the same way clergy have. Whatever sense of covenant the clergy feel will be less without guaranteed appointments. But if that change empowers congregations to take more responsibility for their pastoral leadership, the benefits outweigh the costs.

Itineracy

Behind the guaranteed appointment debate is the larger issue of itineracy, including the appointive power of bishops. Guaranteed appointments cannot continue when one major result is protecting the job security of ineffective clergy. If, or when, the guaranteed appointment ends, the itineracy as currently practiced will be more open to challenge. It is crucial to remember that the itinerant appointment system began as a missional strategy.

The reality is that now there is no one practice of itineracy but multiple expressions of itineracy practiced side by side. On one end of a continuum are the very largest churches, where the role of laity is prominent, with some even forming search committees and, with the permission of the bishop, seeking candidates. On the other end are the very smallest churches where district superintendents are often on their own to find persons to serve those churches, usually local pastors or laity. In between, there are many elders who fall into what a few conferences name as "limited itineracy," in which for various reasons the geographic range of itineration is limited. So to talk of our system of itineracy is to ignore all its variations. The final authority of the bishop to fix appointments is the one common denominator.

The introduction of mandatory consultation into the appointive process formalized what the wisest bishops and superintendents had practiced for years, even in times when the formal process was hidden and authoritarian. The best appointments have always been made when the gifts of clergy and the needs of congregations were known and applied. The concept of every church having a pastor and every pastor a congregation makes such sensitive appointment making virtually impossible for many clergy and churches each year.

There is one model, if applied to all appointments, that would make itineracy work for decades to come. The model, often used in the very largest churches, takes very seriously congregational interests, the interests of potential new pastors, and the bishop's final authority to appoint. For such a system to work, the congregational role would need to become far more prominent (and thus their ownership and engagement as well) while freeing valuable episcopal and superintendent time. At the same time, just knowing that congregations have a stronger role in appointments would increase clergy engagement.

Leader selection shaped by the vision sought

Any conversation about leadership must begin with where we are trying to go and what we want to accomplish. The United Methodism we seek fifteen years from now needs to shape the leaders we seek now. The next question explores the leadership we need for churches of various sizes and types to accomplish the United Methodist witness we envision. There are some essential characteristics for all clergy leadership, but distinctive gifts and experience are needed for different types of churches found in the annual conference.

Such an analysis could be a step toward moving the work of boards of ordained ministry to a proactive stance in which the conference names what it needs more specifically than now is the case.

Focus: New churches

Not only has the annual conference been the center of new church initiatives historically, but it remains the place where the primary leadership for new churches should be lodged because of the conference's mandate to steward and extend the United Methodist witness within its bounds. There are general church roles for research, national priorities, accountability, and training, but these will continue to be in support of what is primarily an annual conference strategy.

New church starts are one of the most effective means of reaching new populations. As the age of churches grows, the proportion experiencing growth declines. In 1906, one-half of the 57,087 congregations in the six predecessor denominations of The United Methodist Church were less than twenty-five years old; today, most United Methodist churches are more than one hundred years old.[5] Existing churches alone cannot increase attendance in proportion to population growth. The only means by which denominations can possibly keep pace with population growth is through new church starts. The correlation between the new church start rate and percentage of membership change is strong.[6]

Where to place new churches?

Denominations must maintain a vital balance in which they continue to focus on their strengths at the same time that they expand their constituencies. Ignoring or devaluing areas of traditional strength makes no sense. The goal is to leverage resources from areas of strength to extend outreach. In promoting a rural strategy when the United States was moving westward and growing increasingly rural, Bishop Asbury used a phrase similar to what he used to advocate for the poor when he sought resources from the established urban areas for the frontier missions. He said we "must draw resources from the centre to the circumference."[7]

In the United States, United Methodism has tended to do better among whites and African Americans; in nonmetropolitan areas; and since the mid-nineteenth century, among more middle- to upper-middle-class people. There are historical and sociological factors for this pattern, but new patterns call for new efforts by these traditional constituencies to expand the circle. Targeting areas for new church starts requires great care, recognizing that population growth is an important, though not the only, factor to consider. Keeping a healthy balance between traditional and emerging constituencies is one essential consideration.

New churches also need to address the striking lack of alignment between centers of population and churches. The top forty U.S. metropolitan areas comprising 50 percent of the population in 2010 are home to only 20 percent of United Methodist churches and 24 percent of members.[8]

What kinds of new churches?

Recently I have been involved in studies of United Methodist new church starts during a twenty-year period for eight annual conferences.[9] The size of new churches after five or more years shows a large percentage (just over half) in the small-church-size tier of 125 or fewer in worship.

In order for the denomination to grow and reach new disciples, more new churches need to grow larger. If the goal is to reach more people, younger people, and more diverse people, we must recognize that since 1975, the group of churches consistently doing all three has been churches averaging 500 or more in worship. In 1975 these churches represented 1 percent of churches and about 8 to 9 percent of membership and attendance. In 2009 they represented 2 percent of churches and

- 25 percent of membership,
- 21 percent of attendance,
- 25 percent of professions of faith,
- 28 percent of youth,
- 31 percent of children, and
- 28 percent of people of color.

An inevitable tension between new church starts and existing churches

In considering the role of the annual conference in new church starts, one cannot avoid the dilemma conferences face in making the case for new churches when hundreds of existing churches become emptier each year. Conferences must take seriously the complex interplay between new and existing churches. Existing churches are of mixed minds. They often resist the conference using resources to start new churches, when existing churches are also in need. At the same time, they recognize the great contribution, both in people and in resources, that churches started in just the recent decades are already making to the United Methodist witness in their conference. On their best days, they also recall that every existing church was once a new church start.

It would be nice to say to existing churches that a new church start means no negative impact on them. Our research shows that existing United Methodist churches in the area of new church starts do show some loss in attendance once the new church begins. Several variables affect the degree of impact. One of the most important is population size. A new church in a large metropolitan area tends to have minimal impact on other churches, whereas a new church start in a smaller community may have much more impact.

The most important finding for the annual conference's mission to steward and extend the United Methodist witness is that new churches and existing churches combined to reach more people than if there were no new church started in the area. Given an increase in population, new churches reach new people at a higher rate than established churches do. Existing churches alone cannot increase attendance in proportion to population growth. The only means by which the denomination can possibly keep pace with population growth is through new church starts.

Focus: Equipping

Since vital congregations are the heart of faithful and fruitful witness, the annual conference also has a role in such vitality for existing churches, but a much more modest role than it has in new church starts. The role of the annual conference is lessened when it comes to equipping congregations based both on the calling of the conference and on the chances for impact by the conference.

Bishops, district superintendents, and conference staff are not the primary stewards of congregational vitality. Churches have pastors and lay leaders for that role. The conference can encourage and support the use of comprehensive programs or strategies for congregations, such as the Call to Action elements of effective pastoral leadership that include aspects of management, visioning, and inspiration; multiple small groups and programs for children and youth; a mix of traditional and contemporary services; and a high percentage of engaged laity who assume leadership roles.[10] One of the programs most used today is *Five Practices of Fruitful Congregations* by Bishop Robert Schnase, built around radical hospitality, passionate worship, intentional faith development, risk-taking mission and service, and extravagant generosity.[11] Some conferences have their own versions of congregational vitality plans that are quite remarkable. Some invest in coaching, mentoring, small groups, and specialized training for revitalization. All of these efforts can help and certainly send the right signals about the expectations of the conference.

But nothing will change until the local leadership determines the need to change. Local leaders have to address what must be done or at least what help they need to do fruitful ministry in their current context. An unfortunate tendency for many United Methodist clergy is to live mentally and emotionally in a future that will be better, rather than focus on hard work in the present. Similarly, congregations are tempted to live in the future. Knowing that they always have the opportunity to request a new pastor, and whether they request one or not, they are likely to get a new pastor fairly regularly, laity often will see the next pastoral move as their strategy for revitalization.

Annual conferences are often thwarted in their best efforts by such unspoken dynamics. Conferences must continue in their equipping efforts but with realism about the inherent limitations of this change theory, given the plethora of other variables at play. Staying attentive to several strategies can strengthen such efforts:

Avoid grandiose goals

There is a difference between visionary goals and illusions. Sometimes we think that if we exaggerate the goal, we will accomplish more. The usual effect is for people not to take the grandiose goal seriously and continue business as usual. Instead of setting goals that are challenging, though seemingly modest, we are inclined more to the dramatic. Instead of saying we will reach more people next year than this year, we say we will double our membership in so many years. Not only do we miss the goal; we do not even stop the loss. Here is an example of such a grand goal:

> Every local church will have at least one
> profession of faith during the year.

Each year about 40 percent of United Methodist churches have no professions of faith. This is tragic, and the desire to change this reality is right.

However, 99 percent of those churches are smaller-attendance churches, so the announced goal is for a subset of churches.

A better goal might be:

We will have more professions of faith next year than this year.

Begin from strength and passion

If the goal is reaching more people through professions of faith, it is wise to begin with those churches with a demonstrated ability to have professions of faith and work from there. The usual tendency is to come up with a program for those with no professions of faith. There are many reasons for beginning where there are strength and passion. Affirming these churches makes it less likely their work will slip, in which case their losses would offset any gains elsewhere. They also know what is working for them and can be a resource for other churches. Since there will be strength and passion around professions of faith in churches of all sizes, types, and locations, their availability to help churches in comparable situations is immense.

The philosophy here is much like the situation churches face each year as they think about their income for the coming year. While all are invited and encouraged to give, the focus cannot be on people who have never made a gift. They are part of the effort, some will give for the first time, and some of them will eventually become generous disciples. But if next year's goal is met, it will come primarily from current contributors giving again and a number of them giving more.

Avoid "Every church will"

"Every church will" is a phrase that no longer serves us well. It calls forth instinctive resistance from some. But even more damaging is the toll the phrase takes on leaders who must cajole participation by the 20 percent least likely to respond.

A better approach is to provide opportunities for all, encourage some, but pressure none. When this principle is combined with the one above, leadership can focus attention on those whose participation is most critical—those where there are strength and passion—instead of on those who do not want to participate. At the same time, this approach is very democratic in that it is offered to everyone, and those places where there is passion but no strength will "lift their hands" immediately. Leadership now can give them more attention.

In this approach, leadership attention shifts dramatically from those with no strength or passion for the subject to those able or at least ready to move forward. Energy needs to go to those ready to engage. What about the others? The reality is that if there is not some degree of desire and readiness on the part of a pastor or congregation, nothing much will happen even if they nominally participate in the program. This is not a judgment on the congregation. In fact, the same congregation with no interest in one initiative may be eager for another.

Great care needs to go into the work of identifying the challenges, and churches, to engage at any one time, since any chance for influence depends on sufficient focus that will limit the universe of conversation. The criterion used to focus must always relate directly to the conference stewardship of the United Methodist witness. Places to look for willing partners are where the United Methodist witness is most at stake, including churches with opportunity unrealized, churches vulnerable without new directions, areas in which no United Methodist church reaches at least one hundred in worship,[12] and churches on the verge of becoming mono-generational.[13]

Focus: Connecting

A first step in rethinking the connecting role of the conference must be a change in perspective about giving, particularly as it relates to apportionments. In addition, the conference must resist the expectation of conformity among its congregations and encourage innovation. Only then can it be effective in facing the new context of the church.

Celebrate success

The church, at all levels, does a poor job of saying "thank you" to people for their financial giving. So an appropriate step is for church leaders at all levels to celebrate giving and payment of apportionments as one of the great success stories of The United Methodist Church. Saying "thank you" often and reporting stories of changed lives through such giving will set the right tone with people who share the vast ministry of The United Methodist Church.

It is important to invite and encourage people to continue their giving, but not with the impression that this topic is the one we are most monitoring and in which we are most interested, which is the impression of many attending our churches today. While many goals are encouraged for churches, no other goal gets the same scrutiny by church leaders as apportionments. My concern is not with the value of paying apportionments but with the unspoken message we convey to clergy and congregations about what really matters, thus making everything else of lesser importance.

The goal of full payment stays the same, but why do we focus on the one thing we do so well while ignoring those things with which we struggle? For example, apportionments may come in at 90 percent in a conference. Is there any conference where 90 percent of the churches end the year with as many or more members than at the beginning of the year? As many in attendance? As many professions of faith? As many children and youth?

The percentage of churches that pay 100 percent of their apportionments each year is far higher than the percentage of churches that raise 100 percent of their local church budgets each year. Almost no entity collects 100 percent of its stated budget. Assuming 100 percent payment of apportionments may be unrealistic for any church judicatory. Furthermore, the effort that goes into pushing the payment rate higher may not be the most efficient use of time, since usually there are many more variables at play in whether churches pay their apportionments than just whether they desire to pay them.

The problem is not with emphasizing apportionments but the inordinate preoccupation we have with them. One way to take pressure off apportionments is for the annual conference to see itself not so much as doing ministry on behalf of others whose role is to fund the ministry. Its role, rather, is to equip and connect congregations with opportunities for mission with primary funding coming out of the initiative and passion generated at the local level because of the power of the need.

The "connection for ministry" in the future will change for the annual conference as well as the general church. There will continue to be ministries best done at the cooperative level beyond the local church, but those are likely to decline dramatically. The Nothing but Nets and Imagine No Malaria efforts to eliminate malaria in Africa by providing lifesaving nets exemplify how denominational leadership can enlist church and secular engagement and funding. The results are much greater than would have been possible through a program totally funded through apportioned giving. The resources and personnel needed to make such an expansive undertaking possible are still significant, though modest in terms of the dollars and service unleashed.

Resist conformity

Gil Rendle provides a reminder of the impact of increasing diversity and new models for church required to reach emerging generations. While congregational expressions of the United Methodist witness in the United States have varied widely from the beginning, the "wilderness is about to become even messier," says Rendle.[14] By that he means that congregations will need much more leeway in how they develop their ministries, even as they are bound by a common identity. The definition of what it means to be connected in spirit and service cannot mean conformity. A much more expansive and generous understanding of connectional suits this era.

In a time when denominational identity accounted for the majority of church choice decisions, insisting on a plethora of expectations for what a "good United Methodist church" looked like may have made sense. Today the advantages of conformity are far outweighed by the necessity to develop indigenous expressions of faith that fit the communities served. The center of connection continues to be the identity, mission, and values discussed in chapter 3, General Church. But just as the General Conference needs to give annual conferences more flexibility, likewise both the General Conference and the annual conference must provide more room for innovation and entrepreneurship among congregations.

CHAPTER 5

Congregations

Leadership is more than doing things well. If a church is carrying out its ministries well, there must be good leadership and vitality, right? Not necessarily. Many declining churches are very accomplished and conscientious in the performance of their activities. Doing things well is far better than not doing them well, but something more is required for vital congregations. In fact, some have described the phase in a church's life when it is still strong but at a plateau as the "performance stage"[1] because its reputation and following come from performing its work better than other churches, even as fewer participate. This stage may be similar to the market-leading company discussed in the introduction that kept improving its offerings while others began to meet the needs of changing constituencies in the marketplace. Even as the established company looked down on its upstart competitors for offering products it considered of lesser quality, many of the upstarts surpassed the market leader by their ability to connect with the needs of more people.

Leaders who understand the dangers of the performance stage are in a better position to lead their congregations to vitality. Fruitful leadership is no more the collection of tasks done well than a sermon is the collection of preparation tasks done well. Doing the sermon preparation tasks well gives a wonderful foundation for a sermon, but a sermon that connects Scripture with the needs of people is something that builds upon the preparation and goes beyond it. The result is far more than the collection of the individual preparation tasks, no matter how well that preliminary work was done.

Mission

"What is our mission?" is the first question for any congregation. A congregation is fortunate to have a good mission stating clearly what it exists *to do*. But more is necessary. The mission needs broad understanding within the congregation and a dominant role in decision making. Often the mission statement is well crafted, prominently framed on the wall, and even printed on the bulletin. That mission, however, may not guide the congregation. Many long-standing churches today have fine formal mission statements, but the guiding unspoken mission of the church is "to stay as good as we are." More energy is expended preserving *what is* than taking the next faithful step God has for the congregation. "Staying as good as we are" is ultimately an unfaithful stance because the current state of things—no matter how wonderful—is never synonymous with God's ultimate will for a congregation. Churches cherish their past but are called to pray and work to accomplish what God wills for the next chapter.

In addition to mission, core values are essential but do not substitute for mission. Declining churches often fill their mission statements with values that describe the church rather than state its purpose. For example, a congregation whose mission is "to be a loving, caring, and supportive faith community" will find it hard to know what that church is to do next. Values serve both as positive guides for the church's work and as boundaries within which everyone seeks to accomplish the mission. A challenge for congregations is to name their values in a way that reflects their heritage and lifts high standards. Sadly, the most common value named by church members is "friendly." Surely there are more biblically and theologically rich values that distinguish congregations from other organizations, and even other churches, than friendly.

Ministry in a context

Anyone who has guided a group through the process of establishing a mission and values knows that the task can take much time and energy. In the end, everyone feels good about the accomplishment and hopeful about the future of the church. In fact, there is sometimes a tendency to think that a good mission statement and values will make things happen, especially when the mission and values are printed, promoted, and posted prominently.

The reality is that mission statements and values alone accomplish nothing. They come alive as members carry out specific parts of the ministry, but only if they do so with awareness of their particular context. These tasks may not seem grand compared to the mission and values, but it is in the work of many people that the mission and values are embodied. If the mission is accomplished and the values upheld, it will be through concrete ministries of worship, education, missions, and stewardship that connect with the current context of the congregation.

The tendency in mature congregations, such as the overwhelming majority of United Methodist churches in the United States, is to improve the performance of each of their ministry areas. Leaders celebrate the opportunity to improve God's work through this church and contribute to the faith development of many lives through these ministries. Improvements through such good management do indeed advance the mission of the church. But there are limits to good management, and most United Methodist churches ran up against those limits in the past several decades. This is the time churches discover that good practices, even superior practices, are no longer good enough.

No matter how laity and clergy change or improve ministries, the impact of those ministries continues to decline. The problem is that the assumptions on which the ministries began and now continue no longer fit the context of the congregation.

Do our assumptions still fit?

Peter Drucker maintains that most organizational problems are not the result of groups doing things poorly or even doing the wrong things. Organizations fail, he contends, because the assumptions on which the organization developed, and on which it is being run, no longer fit reality.

Could the good practices of our congregations be taking for granted assumptions that were accurate in the past, but no longer fit? Common assumptions among churches shape their ministry, but the reality is changing:

- *People in our communities are religious.* The only religious preference that has grown in every U.S. state since 2001 is "no religion."[2]

- *There are lots of young families with children.* Married couples with children under eighteen living at home represented 50 percent of households in the 1950s; today, only 21 percent.[3]

- *Most adults are married.* Married couples now make up just under 50 percent of households in the United States.[4]

- *Young adults get married in their twenties and early thirties and return to church.* Married people are more likely to attend church; but of young adults between twenty-five and thirty-five, just over half are single.

- *Most people in our community already attend a church.* The percentage of unchurched people has increased in virtually every part of the United States in recent years. Polls still show that over 40 percent of people worship each week, but actual attendance numbers do not back that up.[5]

- *Many people have moved away.* This is true in some areas, but churches can be too quick to jump to conclusions. Often the children of church members have moved away; but there are new residents, often less well off, who have moved in. How else does a new church succeed in a building once used by a congregation that died because "all the people have moved away"? People moving from one state to another is at a sixty-year low.[6]

- *If new people are interested, they will join the church.* Many people today participate actively in church without joining for quite some time, if ever.[7]

- *Most new members will come from our denomination.* There was a time when newcomers found the nearest church of their denomination to attend. Denomination matters much less today, while a church's vision, ministries, and relationships count for far more.[8]

Assumptions shape decisions about ministry. The mission must be lived within the current context, and good leaders name the reality of the context accurately. Lay and clergy leaders will be wise to examine their assumptions and compare them with the current data about their context.

Focus

As with other expressions of denominational life, local churches face the challenge of focus. In the early years of a new congregation, attention is narrowly focused on connecting with people in the community, providing inspired worship services, and building relationships that hold people together. As time goes by and the church develops a host of administrative, pastoral, program, and physical needs, attention becomes more broadly dispersed. Churches begin to decline when they lose the power of focused vision and come to see "doing ministry" as performing all the countless tasks needed to maintain the church.

At every chapter in a congregation's life, it must clarify the few things most important for it to take the next faithful step. The other tasks will still be done, but now everything must be viewed through the lens of the vision; that is, the form that the mission takes in this particular chapter, given the church's context. Without such deliberate reconsideration that takes account of the church's identity and its changing environment, decline is inevitable.

Dan Aleshire, executive director of the Association of Theological Schools in the United States and Canada, went back to his hometown in Ohio to chronicle the ways in which the churches of the community had changed since his family moved there fifty years before. One church was Concord United Methodist Church. Concord was located in open country when Dan was growing up there. The farms that once surrounded the church have been replaced by subdivisions and strip malls. The Concord church building still stands as it did with its stained glass windows and steeple but now as the Concord Chapel Pet Hospital. Aleshire notes that there are thriving United Methodist churches in the area, but "this picture postcard of a church must have been slow stepping when the dance called for quick-quick."[9]

What do thriving and vital congregations do that other churches do not, often within the same community? After observing churches for many years, I have noticed that the most vital congregations seem always to do two things. They connect with their communities, and they connect people with God, especially through worship experiences. Each supports and makes possible the other.

Therefore, the following are areas worthy of focus for congregations as we prepare for the challenges of the future:

Connect people with God

"Churches whose primary concern is making people full of God," say Kirk Hadaway and David Roozen, "are also churches whose pews will be full of people."[10] No congregation can be vital apart from a lively and ongoing experience of God's presence in the lives of its constituents. It is from this powerful relationship with God's spirit that all else flows. As John Wesley put it, "Set your heart firm on [God], and on other things only as they are in and from [God]."[11] There is no congregational vitality disconnected from the source of power.

If the church does not have a spiritual message communicated contextually with energy and integrity, it has nothing to offer to a world searching for hope amidst despair. The problem is not people's lack of interest in God. Living in every community are people seeking the abundant life possible only through alignment of life with God's will. It is easy to decry the sources to which people turn for spiritual guidance, but that reality may mean that others are doing a better job of addressing the religious needs of our neighbors. The question for churches is whether we have a word for them. There are more churches today than ever and more people searching for hope for their lives.

Worship is primary

To glorify God and to share God as revealed in Jesus Christ are at the heart of why any church exists. Worship is where both longtime members are nourished and new persons come to faith. The church is much more than worship, but without vital worship attendance, it is not likely that members are growing and new disciples are being reached. Also, worship attendance is perhaps the one factor where improvement tends to help every other part of the church's ministry. Churches reaching more people, younger people, and more diverse people today spend far more time on worship planning, preparation, and evaluation than is the pattern in most mainline churches. Worship is not everything the church does, but it is primary and other things flow from it.

If a church succeeds in reaching more people in worship when the pattern has been one of decline, then a different church emerges and is on its way to a new day. If a church continues to focus on everything, success is not likely. Improved worship attendance can make a difference throughout the congregation. Also, worship attendance is perhaps the most egalitarian metric to use. All people count, and all churches are located where there are people not in church.

The worship recession

It is commonplace to hear references to what it means for churches to function in the current financial recession. But another recession going on in the United States has been affecting churches far longer and more consistently than the economic downturn. It is the worship recession.

The United Methodist Church, like many other denominations, is currently in the midst of a worship recession. Worship attendance did relatively well in the 1990s, with increases in some years. However, beginning in 2002, there have been major declines every year.

Figures below from four denominations show how relatively strong attendance was in the closing years of the 1990s compared to the opening years of the 2000s.[12]

Worship Attendance Change		
	1994–2000	**2001–2008**
Episcopal Church	+3.39%	-17.86%
United Methodist Church	+2.53%	-10.22%
Evangelical Lutheran Church in America	-0.58%	-15.41%
Presbyterian Church (U.S.A.)	-2.76%	-15.62%
Average	**+2.58%**	**-14.78%**

People in the United States flocked to houses of worship in unusually high numbers following the September 11, 2001, attacks. Some say this attendance surge lasted about five weeks. However long it was, it did not result in long-term attendance gains. The opposite actually happened among many churches.

How do new people view a church?

The Lewis Center for Church Leadership asked church members in several states to attend nearby churches as visitors and report on their findings. Many findings reflect the difficulty churches have in viewing things from the perspective of persons new to their church. The challenge is to think of everything from arrival to departure from the perspective of someone who has never been to the church before. This new perspective will shape signage, the bulletin, the work of greeters, and a host of other things. Attention to such details can address the worship recession and the loss of opportunity to reach new disciples.

Signage. Most visitors found directional signage inadequate. It is useful for a congregation to do this exercise: ask some people to do a "drive in and walk through" as if they had never been to the church before. Was it easy to find the church? Is the entrance clear? Is there visitor parking? Are there greeters near where people park? Is it obvious what door to enter for worship? Are there directions to the nursery and restrooms? When a congregation adds signage, current members will hardly notice, but newcomers will immediately recognize that the church is expecting them.

Culture of hospitality. Although visitors were welcomed upon arrival, usu-ally by the official greeters and the pastor, those sitting around them did not greet the visitors. Members need to see themselves as the hosts of Christ. A good host knows that the most important person is the stranger or the one left alone. Another sign of hospitality is providing guest parking. This is a strong signal that the church has new people attending and is expecting guests.

The worship service. Visitors found some parts of the service confusing. Many did not grow up in church and were unfamiliar with worship practices. If there is a part of the worship that most members know from memory, the bul-letin can indicate the page number where people can find it, or it can be printed. Guests will appreciate this thoughtfulness. If people are to stand at a particular time, it can be indicated in the bulletin or by a lifted hand by the wor-ship leader. Simple instructions for Communion and other parts of the service can help bring on board those who are new. When church leaders walk through the entire service as someone coming to church for the first time, they may dis-cover what will make it easier for new people to participate and to feel at home.

Congregational participation. *Liturgy* means "the work of the people." Visitors report a high energy level among most worship leaders but not so much within the congregations themselves. Music and singing may increase everyone's engagement. Choirs need to remember that leading and enhancing congregational singing may be their most important function. If attendance is far below the sanctuary's seating capacity, some portion can be roped off. Paying special attention to times in the service when engagement is highest will give an opportunity to build upon those times. Reducing time gaps and staying on schedule will help hold people's attention.

Involvement of younger people. Many visitors observed how few younger people were in worship leadership. Churches can brainstorm various ways of involving people across all ages in worship responsibilities. Having younger people visible in worship will be noticed by current members and new people. Creativity in involving younger people will be important.

Focus: Connect with your community

Fall in love with the community again

Although no *one* thing is the absolute key to reengaging a people-centered ministry in our churches, one practice that could go a long way toward that goal is for churches to fall in love with their communities again.

The longer a church has been in existence, the less knowledgeable it is likely to be about its community and the less connected it becomes with that community. That sounds strange, yet it is rare that a long-existing church is more aware of the trends, demographics, and movements of its community than a new congregation in that same place.

How does this happen? In the early years, a congregation gives careful attention to the community, its people, and their needs. Otherwise, it does not survive. Then the congregation reaches a point of critical mass. Weeks or months go by without new members joining, and the congregation continues to stay alive. Often there is a shift in focus from reaching new disciples to caring for current members.

Many congregations become worlds unto themselves, lacking active engagement with the changes in their surroundings. This movement from external sensitivity to internal focus occurs in virtually all organizations. Without a careful plan to stay close to the heartbeat of one's surroundings, internal considerations dominate. Good leaders seek to link the internal life of the congregation and its external context.

Without the outside, there is no inside. Congregations are not started to care for themselves but to serve others. Without attention to bridging the outside/inside gap, congregations forget their original purpose and turn in upon themselves.

Churches exist to serve

During hard times especially, churches can forget their purpose and heritage. Forgetting our original mission can easily happen under the pressure to survive. Churches conduct a financial audit each year. What if each church conducted a mission audit once a year to assess its faithfulness to the Wesleyan tradition of serving others? Only one question is required in this audit, which comes from United Methodist pastor Don Haynes:

> If your church closed today, who would miss it
> other than your members?

Members might make a list of the people and groups in the community outside the membership who would miss the church. What would they miss? They could repeat the exercise a year later. Is the list longer or shorter?

It is in answering such a question that we may discover clues about the current state of our church. We may come to see some reasons for our strength or weakness as a faithful community of fruitful disciples.

Albert Outler describes evangelism in the Wesleyan spirit as Wesley teaching his followers to be a band of "martyrs and servants," emptying themselves as servants, giving themselves freely for others.[13] Thriving and serving were indeed linked. The growth of the Wesleyan enterprise is directly related to its identification with the needs of all God's children.

Is this happening today? Are people saying that because our church is in the community, there are no hungry people? Are people saying that because of our church's presence in the community, there is no bigotry or discrimination? Are they saying because we are in the community, there is no one homeless? Such questions continue to be the test for heirs of the Wesleyan spirit.[14]

Mission as the emerging entry point for new people

It is intriguing that the first connection people have with a congregation tends to change from time to time.

For churches with struggling adult Sunday schools, it may be hard to imagine that for a long time the Sunday school was the most likely church entry point for most adults, as well as children and youth. Well into the 1950s in many denominations and regions, the most common invitation church members gave their new neighbors or coworkers was to attend their Sunday school class with them. It was not uncommon for church school attendance to run higher than worship attendance.

Most of us are more familiar with the pattern that came next, in which the most likely first connection with a congregation was a worship service. Church members inviting others to attend their church would now more likely invite them to "worship with us." In this period the worship attendance in most churches pulled ahead, sometimes well ahead, of Sunday school attendance.

We may be on the verge of another change, in which the entry point to a congregation for more and more people is through service and mission. This seems especially true for the young. For many young people, inviting their friends who do not attend church to "come to my church" may not be the most comfortable invitation to make or the one most likely to receive a positive response. On the other hand, few young people are reluctant to invite their friends to join them for a service project sponsored by the church, and few young people will turn down such an invitation.

It is too early to know whether mission as an entry point to church will take hold in the way that Sunday school and worship did in prior times. But we do know that for increasing numbers of persons with a passion to serve and some disillusionment with the church, mission may be their most likely entry point—if churches are actually serving others and including new people in such service.

Looking to the Future

Faithful laity and clergy work diligently every day to be in ministry through The United Methodist Church. The faithfulness and diligence, however, do not always lead to fruitfulness. We know too well that many congregations are in decline and too many are in crisis.

The questions suggested in the congregation reset section of chapter 2 are a starting point for assessing what is currently going on in a church. The invitation to examine the working assumptions of a congregation can be another significant step. Then comes the necessity of looking at the life of a congregation from the view of an outsider, who may better be called a potential disciple— yearning for good news.

None of these steps can guarantee the turnaround of a declining congregation. But without them it is unlikely that we are providing the foundation for revitalization. We know that God gives the growth, and we continue to be called to do the planting and watering.

CHAPTER 6

Reaching More People, Younger People, More Diverse People

United Methodism's Twenty-First-Century Challenge

Most of United Methodism's dilemmas today are a mixture of technical and adaptive challenges. With technical challenges, the problem and solution are known, and the task is implementation. But with adaptive challenges, the problem is uncertain, the solution is uncertain, or both are uncertain. Resetting the financial baseline is technical at one level, yet requires tremendous adaptive capabilities to enact. Adaptive change always requires new learning and fresh ways of engaging one's context. In the end, technical changes alone are not sufficient for the ultimate goal of a vibrant Wesleyan witness—one that has the movement quality of our predecessors. There is one looming adaptive challenge that we can address only through major learning, innovation, and the wisdom of everyone through Christian conferencing.

The United Methodist Church in the United States has a future only to the extent that it can find ways to reach more people, younger people, and more diverse people. This phrase originated with an annual conference planning process I was asked to lead. A survey of conference leaders identified issues of importance, such as reversing declining membership, addressing financial loads, reaching younger people, engaging communities, and reaching out in evangelism. As a leadership council gathered to establish priorities, small groups addressed this task: if you now go to five churches to tell their leaders "what the priority is for the coming years," which of the issues named would make the people more hopeful for their church? Each group named the same priority: "reaching younger people." "Reaching young people" would not have worked. But reaching younger people fit the vast differences in churches and communities. It carried hope and, if successful, would improve other concerns they listed.

From this remarkable consensus emerged the phrase "reaching more people, younger people, and more diverse people," now commonplace among United Methodists. It was named in "Ten Provocative Questions for The United Methodist Church" prepared for the Council of Bishops in 2007.[1] From that, a bishop asked gatherings of laity and clergy to identify the one question most critical to the future of the United Methodist witness in their state. Every group selected the same question: Can the church change to reach more people, younger people, and more diverse people?

The Church's New Frontier

The United Methodist Church did very well growing up with the United States through the nineteenth century and into the early decades of the twentieth century. Then as the twentieth century unfolded, the nation changed, but the church did not. Earlier generations followed Americans from East to West, from urban to frontier, and from lower to middle and upper-middle classes. But success led to staying with practices even as they became increasingly less effective.

Today The United Methodist Church in the United States is not only dramatically smaller, but it is older and less diverse than the population. Thus, the premise emerges that we must learn to reach more people, younger people, and more diverse people.

In thinking of these three categories, some may find themselves identifying with one or perhaps two of them. My observation is that United Methodists either will successfully achieve all three goals or will achieve none. They are inextricably linked. If we reach more people, they are likely to be younger, since United Methodists are overrepresented in every age category of fifty and above and underrepresented in every age category under age fifty, the age of the vast majority of the population. Likewise, if we reach more people, they likely will be more diverse. Our denomination is vastly overrepresented among white people compared to their presence in the population and underrepresented in every other racial group, at a time when diversity is growing. If we reach younger people, they are likely to be more diverse since the younger population is vastly more diverse than the nation's older population.[2]

These statistics make clear whom we are *not* reaching for Christ. They tell us that as we respond to the call to take the good news to all people, we must give special attention to younger people and more diverse people. United Methodists have expressed a commitment to reaching these underrepresented constituencies. We must learn now to link such commitments to accountability for our action and fruitfulness.

Reaching More People

The $6 billion enigma

In The United Methodist Church on the first day of a new year, more than thirty-three thousand congregations begin working toward a common mission: to make disciples of Jesus Christ for the transformation of the world. In addition to the congregations, there are about eight million members and the most educated clergy in the denomination's history. These congregations average more than $1.7 million in assets, plus they are part of a denomination with a multitude of agencies and institutions. But if all this were not enough to accomplish the mission, The United Methodist Church has available more than $6 billion in new money that will be given and spent during the year to accomplish the mission. Still, at the end of the year, there is not a net gain of a single person who seeks to begin the life of discipleship through The United Methodist Church. This is not to say that significant things are not happening throughout the denomination. Lives are changed and people helped around the world because of the United Methodist witness. But it remains significant that we are using massive amounts of resources without expanding the Wesleyan witness or even holding our own.

John Wesley had a passion for all humanity to come to know the love of God revealed in Jesus Christ. Many congregations claim the mission of "making disciples" but need to align their ministry to connect new disciples with new life in Christ and to help all grow in their discipleship. If current members are growing in discipleship, which includes witness, surely many will come to faith in Christ through such witness.

Natural decrease

Demographers speak of natural decrease occurring when a county or state has more deaths than births. For example, in the 2010 census, estimates show one in four U.S. counties experiencing natural decrease. Sometimes these counties are referred to as dying counties, a reminder that species cease to exist when there are more deaths than births. Those living in counties experiencing natural decrease quickly see the negative impact on schools, medical care, and business. Such counties were rare in the United States until the 1960s, when the baby boom surge in births ended.[3]

What would be the equivalent of natural decrease in the church? One way to think about it would be to compare the number of people coming to faith in Jesus Christ each year in congregations compared to those dying. Traditionally churches experience far more professions of faith than deaths, but the trend is downward among United Methodist churches.

Year	Professions of Faith	Deaths	Difference[4]
1968	261,832	113,492	148,340
1980	209,894	120,000	89,894
1990	196,628	121,467	75,161
2000	196,928	120,348	76,580
2009	148,446	100,901	47,545

Each congregation would do well to examine the figures for their church.

Reaching Younger People

Early American Methodists could have focused only on the needs of existing adult members. They chose instead to give attention to the future and to the young. Their passion for establishing colleges is a prime example. Various youth and young adult organizations and movements played key roles in the development of vigorous leadership for the church. The Sunday school movement was a major effort toward the evangelization and education of new generations of Christians.

Today the failure to reach younger people is abundantly clear. Recent research shows that while clergy and laity want younger people, congregational leaders are not willing to change their worship or budgets to reach younger generations. The research illustrates that the gap between rhetoric and action is as large as the age gap that some believe threatens the future viability of the denomination.[5] Erwin McManus, pastor of Mosaic Church in Los Angeles, captured the reality of churches unwilling to change when he said, "Churches all across the country have decided they love their traditions more than their children."[6]

The task is not easy. The dilemma faced by most church leaders today is to reach younger generations who see the world in fundamentally different ways than the older generations already in the church. But the church's future requires finding new ways to address multiple generations.

One dramatic indicator of this aging trend in The United Methodist Church is the sharp decline in the number of young clergy. The percentage of young elders went from over 20 percent in the 1970s to under 5 percent by 2005. Fortunately, since 2005 the percentage has held steady, with modest gains to 5.6 percent in 2011.[7] A study of all under-thirty-five clergy, including elders, deacons, and local pastors, found that their most common characteristics were active involvement in church as children and youth. The congregation was the context in which they heard their call, and the pastor was a key mentor. It is unrealistic to assume that efforts to enlist young clergy can succeed so long as the places where the call is most nurtured continue to reach fewer young people.[8]

Annual conferences

What can we learn from annual conferences reaching younger people?

- Reach new populations, which tend to be younger and more diverse than traditional United Methodist constituents.

- Begin new congregations, which generally reach new populations and younger populations at a higher rate than existing churches.

- Help existing congregations increase their worship attendance. The higher the worship attendance of a congregation, the more likely it is to reach younger populations.

- Strengthen those ministries most directly touching younger people, such as children, youth, young adult, camping, and campus ministries.

Local churches

The uncomfortable reality is that younger people have problems with the church today that include, but go far beyond, matters of worship style and music. Many young people are deeply uncomfortable with what they think the church represents. Adam Hamilton, pastor of the United Methodist Church of the Resurrection, preached the sermon series "When Christians Get It Wrong," later published as a book with the same name. Doing this series took courage. Adam named sore spots for youth and young adults about the church, and in doing so, he laid bare some all-too-common church practices and attitudes.[9]

Such bold yet sensitive leadership is essential to reach emerging generations. It is tempting to blame the young for decreased participation. But recent research shows there are reasons younger persons either stay away or fall away from the church. These reports also indicate positive directions for the future.[10]

While young persons are not hostile to religion, faith serves more as a backdrop to their lives than as something central. Christian Smith and Melissa Denton describe the theological world of the young as Moralistic Therapeutic Deism (MTD) because it has little to do with God or a sense of a divine mission in the world. MTD is a spirituality of having personal happiness and helping people treat each other well. It offers comfort, bolsters self-esteem, and helps solve problems by encouraging people to do good and feel good while keeping God at arm's length. The research finds that, rather than abandoning their parents' faith, young people developed this mind-set precisely from their parents, often with the help of their churches.[11]

Common themes emerge across various studies of the current state of youth and their religious preferences:

- Youth ministry matters. Youth ministry must go beyond entertainment to address what youth are seeking: belonging, community, meaning, and purpose beyond themselves.

- Parents matter. The relationship between solid faith by parents and youth is strong, and both children's and youth ministry now recognize that parents must be partners in the faith formation of new generations.

- Congregations must recover their theological voice. Youth have a fuzzy theology precisely because many of their churches do. The church must invite the young to join the effort to rediscover faith that sparks missional imagination.

While the goal of ministering to a younger constituency is essential, there is never only one value or goal at stake. The goal of reaching younger persons cannot be accomplished unless it is achieved in a manner consistent with other core values. In a church with multiple generations, there will always be tension. Such tension can be healthy and a sign of life, signaling that the congregation has a future. Within its own values, the church has the resources to help it serve existing members while reaching emerging generations. To focus for a time on those most missing does not mean others are neglected. It is simply the kind of strategic concern the good shepherd shows in giving special attention to the one lost sheep, without forgetting the ninety-nine thaat are not lost.

Reaching More Diverse People

Racial ethnic

Diversity is a key value for United Methodists, and a strong commitment continues toward the elimination of racial inequities. As with all mainline denominations, The United Methodist Church has admirable statements and commitments to inclusiveness and diversity. But not one of the mainline denominations has demonstrated that it can reach any racial group other than white as effectively as it reaches white people.

Diversity was a challenge for Wesley and early Methodists; yet the results make clear the seriousness with which Wesley took the task. The need for a renewed spirit of inclusion of people is crucial today. The United States is experiencing one of the most dramatic shifts in racial and ethnic makeup in its history. The youthfulness of the growing racial ethnic diversity in the United States makes its impact even more significant for the future. The church's vitality in the century ahead will be shaped largely by its willingness and ability to respond to the changing face of the country.

The United States today is going through the greatest increase in racial diversity since the introduction of slavery. While immigration is a part of the increasing diversity, noted demographer William H. Frey maintains that if immigration stopped today, the United States would still see substantial gains in racial ethnic populations for decades to come. The Census Bureau projects that under a "no further immigration" scenario, the racial ethnic population proportion would rise from about 35 percent today to 42 percent in 2050. Most of the increasing racial diversity of the population will come from natural growth among persons already living in the country. Frey also points out that popular conceptions of where people of color live do not always match reality. For example, a majority of all Hispanic, African American, and Asian residents of major metropolitan areas now live in the suburbs.[12]

And how is the church responding to this changed context? Virtually all United Methodist conferences reach people of color less well than they reach whites. A diverse population within the area of a conference usually means more diversity among United Methodists, and conferences that reach a higher percentage of the white population (compared to other conferences) also tend to reach a comparatively higher percentage of people of color. But the percentage of people of color reached is still less than the percentage of whites.[13]

Advances in diversity are possible. The remarkable increases in diversity for internal leadership positions make that clear. Significant changes occurred through careful attention to increasing diversity among bishops, superintendents, agency staff, clergy, and General Conference delegations. A next logical step is to apply the same proved strategy—name the priority, set goals, monitor consistently, ensure accountability—directly to the mission of the denomination to make disciples, thus connecting the value of diversity even more directly with our purpose. One can hardly imagine the change in the United Methodist witness in the United States as a result of a commitment to make disciples of Jesus Christ among the growing populations of color. A compelling case exists for the affirmative action and monitoring priority in the next decade to be professions of faith among people of color.

Economic

As Methodism spread across the United States, the new movement found its following almost entirely among "ordinary people." So it is not unusual that United Methodists see themselves as average Americans, not the richest and not the poorest. If this were once the case, it appears no longer to be so.

United Methodism has taken on an increasingly upper-middle-class character. According to recent research, United Methodists are most represented in the top economic tiers, with gradually declining numbers with each subsequent lower economic tier.

The Research Office of the General Board of Global Ministries used databases to track the presence of United Methodists by zip codes as a way of determining the incomes of members.[14] To measure economic level, median household income (MHI) was used, that income for the entire household at which half the households are higher and half lower. When all zip codes in the United States are ranked from the highest MHI to the lowest, The United Methodist Church locations can be grouped within this ranking and their membership counted with its respective zip codes.

For purposes of this exercise, members are assumed to live in the zip codes where their churches are located. While I know this is not exactly the case, it still gives a way to locate as closely as we can members with their respective zip code categories by income.

When the zip codes are divided by MHI into five equal groups of zip codes from wealthiest to poorest and then United Methodist membership is attributed to each of the quintiles, a distinct pattern emerges. The largest number of United Methodists is found in the top 20 percent of zip codes with the highest MHI. There are not dramatic differences in the number of United Methodists in each of the other quintiles, but the pattern is unmistakable.

After showing the largest membership in the wealthiest zip codes, the numbers of United Methodists consistently get smaller with each subsequent zip code group as incomes become lower. The same pattern of gradual but consistent decline with each less wealthy cohort of zip codes occurs when the zip codes are divided into four or three groupings instead of five.[15]

Marital status

More young families with children

"What we really need is more young families with children." How many times have we heard those familiar words spoken in churches? The image of many young families with children brings memories of a time many churches associate with their heyday decades ago. But there are changed realities to consider if churches want to move forward into the future instead of look back. Most churches are doing as well today in reaching married couples with children as they ever have. But such families represent a dramatically smaller percentage of households today than in the past.

Eighty percent of the U.S. population today does not fit the profile of married couples with children at home. Sociologist Penny Long Marler points out that the 1950s "were a statistical anomaly providing the largest proportional pool of married couples with children in American history."[16] Churches that think of outreach only in terms of young families with children are excluding a large pool of potential new participants. A church targeting married couples with children could potentially reach 20 percent of households. Even by expanding the reach to all married couples, the potential reach is only 50 percent of households.

Households are changing

If we are reaching families with children, then whom are we missing? There are a host of household arrangements today more represented in the population than in churches as the shape of families changes. Reports by the Pew Research Center and the U.S. Census Bureau name some of those changes:[17]

- Decline in marriage. The percentage of married adults dropped from 72 percent in 1960 to just over 50 percent today.

- Delay in marriage. In 1960, 68 percent of all twenty-somethings were married; in 2008, just 26 percent were.

- Rise of single parenting. The percentage of children reared by a single parent was up to 25 percent in 2008 compared to 9 percent in 1960.

- Rise in children living with grandparents. Of the 7.5 million children who lived with a grandparent in 2010, 22 percent did not have a parent present in the household.

- Rise in one-person households. One-person households grew to 27 percent in 2010 from 13 percent in 1960.

While generational differences receive much attention, it is remarkable how people's highest values tend to stay relatively constant from one generation to another. However, the way each new generation expresses those values tends to be different. Even with all the changes in the shape of family and households, people still share a strong commitment to family as a value. According to the Pew report, the vast majority of adults (76 percent) consider their own family to be the most important and most satisfying element of their lives.

Reaching new people is a challenge for most churches. They do not need the extra burden of waiting for people who do not exist to return to church. In the days ahead, churches are most likely to be fruitful in reaching others if they understand who the people around them are and develop ministries and plans to reach those constituencies, especially those represented in their communities but not in their churches.

Who Is Missing?

No persons are more valuable in the eyes of God because of race, age, or other demographic categories. However, the church is called to minister to the people God has given us. Therefore, the changing makeup of the people God has given us in our communities needs to capture our careful attention. While we celebrate and cherish each person already in our congregations, staying attuned to "who is missing" is a way of looking at our mission fields as God sees them.

What Is Ahead for The United Methodist Church?

*O, L*ORD*, I have heard of your renown,*
*and I stand in awe, O L*ORD*, of your work.*
In our own time revive it;
in our own time make it known.

Habakkuk 3:2

What words will best describe twenty-first-century United Methodism? Some words that describe United Methodism in the United States in past centuries might be these:

- Eighteenth century—fervor and marginality

- Nineteenth century—growth and establishment

- Twentieth century—maturity and decline

But what about the twenty-first century?

Denominations, like all organizations, experience life cycles not unlike human beings. For most of the last century, United Methodism in the United States has been a very mature organization, well established but in decline. Great strength comes with maturity. Yet there are particular pitfalls for mature organizations that emerging movements do not face.

In the early days of a movement, there are focused mission and clear vision. There is a good fit between mission and needs. In this time of intense passion, virtually all energy is focused on the vision. Such intense commitment establishes strength and growth. But as we have seen, the most dangerous time for an organization is the time of success. Without ongoing renewal, any organization inevitably struggles to maintain its success. Indeed, decline often follows maturity.

The future does not look bright, but it is in times of hardship that new visions often emerge. It was in a time of despair that Nehemiah and his people united to rebuild the wall. It was after years of suffering that Habakkuk sought and received the vision that the just shall live by faith. In was in the midst of life-denying realities that Jesus proclaimed the vision that all might have abundant life.

Leading between Memory and Vision

Church leaders stand today between a past that is gone and a future that awaits consummation. Not only are we inheritors of God's great acts in history, including the Wesleyan movement; we stand in a present context with many challenges. Biblical accounts of the Babylonian exile offer lessons to today's church leaders living in the tension between a confident past and the still-unfolding promise of God's future. Walter Brueggemann sees exile as a helpful metaphor for the situation of mainline churches today. "The mainline Christian tale has run out in exile." The "ideology of empire" that once fit mainline churches no longer fits. The exile image is more appropriate.[1]

Bruce Birch speaks of people of faith always living and serving between memory and vision.[2] It is not enough for leaders to name the crisis, identify the problems, and document the failures. Leaders draw from the heritage of faith to point with hope toward a new vision from God. Without such a rooted searching for the new thing that God is doing, there can be no hope. Without hope, there can be no energy for transformation.

This hope comes not from a nostalgic return to the empire days of a culture gone. Neither does it come from adopting values alien to God's revelation in Christ. The hope that can lead from weariness to energy is rooted in a God who brings resurrection from death, hope from despair, love from hate, and forgiveness from revenge.

Cornel West speaks of "subversive joy." It is the joy of a people who suffer from many things but possess a joy that makes no logical sense to the world. This joy in the midst of exilic problems is grounded in a source not seen but with the power to liberate us from fear.[3] God's leaders proclaim God's coming new age even when signs are not always apparent. God's leaders help write a new chapter for God's people who have always lived between memory and vision.

We need to remember that there is a lag time between new vision and visible results. If we do not, discouragement and even despair may tempt us to try one quick-fix solution after another in the hope of making rapid changes to situations suffering from years of inattention. No past perceived "golden age" is the standard by which to measure the future. Such golden ages tend to mark the end of an era far more than the era itself. Those celebrated chapters from the past came from efforts years before that never appeared golden but rather chaotic, hard, and painful, as something new emerged.

Legacy Costs and Assets

We know of the tremendous legacy costs The United Methodist Church has in its system of institutions, boards, and practices that come from another era.

Addressing the legacy costs will give us a chance to have a future. But the shape of that future must draw from a much larger set of legacy assets. Indeed, where our legacy costs abound, our legacy assets abound more abundantly:

- We see other churches growing without remembering that Methodism achieved the greatest example of church growth in American history.

- We see new churches springing up in our communities while forgetting that from 1870 to the end of WWI, the churches that make up The United Methodist Church today averaged a net gain of one new church a day for fifty years.

- We watch younger people drawn to churches featuring newer forms of worship and forget that Methodism began with innovative worship practices designed to bring the gospel to the people.

- We forget that our fewer and poorer denominational ancestors started more than one thousand schools, colleges, and universities within one hundred years.

- And even as we seem helpless to respond to the growing racial diversity of the nation, we remember that when Bishop Asbury died, one-fourth of American Methodists were African Americans.

Russell Richey notes the energy, vision, and dynamism found among loyal, committed, and effective leaders in our congregations but contends, "We have tired our people out with too much structure, too much business, too much skirmish, and too much regulation. But the Wesleyan spirit, though walled in, remains very much alive."[4]

We address legacy costs in order to rediscover far richer legacy assets. Otherwise, we will be captive to legacy costs. We make hard choices not to survive but to tame the burden of legacy costs in order to release the far more bountiful legacy assets.

We began with Nehemiah's defining the reality of destroyed gates and walls. Nehemiah did not stop there. He lifted a vision to "rebuild the wall," to which the committed said, "Let us start building!" (Nehemiah 2:17-18). Surely other needs faced Nehemiah and his people, but for the moment, God's call was to rebuild the wall. That is focus. When asked what it took to be a great writer, Robert Penn Warren reportedly said, "A passionate disinterest in a host of worthwhile activities."

Giving New Generations a Chance

The proposals in this book plus other similar options will not produce the new United Methodism worthy of its past. But they will give emerging generations a chance to develop that new movement. Otherwise, the young leaders of today will be left either to become ecclesiastical civil servants of an empire over which the sun is setting or to leave the denomination to join newer movements more nimble and flexible in addressing an utterly changed context.

One marvelous development of recent years is the emergence of new generations of United Methodist leaders steeped in Wesleyan theology and heritage, passionate to share Christ with ever-growing numbers of people of all kinds, and with a commitment to justice for all in an increasingly diverse and global world. They will shape whatever the new expression of the Wesleyan witness will be for the bulk of the twenty-first century—if we do not squander the next decade just trying to sustain things as they are.

Historian William Warren Sweet described John Wesley and Francis Asbury as "prophets of the long road."[5] May God give us such new leaders for a new church in a new day.

Notes

Preface

1. Russell E. Richey, *Methodist Connectionalism: Historical Perspectives* (Nashville: General Board of Higher Education and Ministry, 2009), 52.

Introduction

1. William Warren Sweet, *The Methodists,* vol. 4., *Religion on the American Frontier: 1783–1840* (Chicago: University of Chicago Press, 1946), 3.

2. George R. Crooks, *The Life of Bishop Matthew Simpson* (New York: Harper and Bros., 1890), 394-95. Not many years later, President Ulysses S. Grant "remarked that there were three great parties in the United States: the Republican, the Democratic, and the Methodist Church." Richard J. Carwardine, "Methodists, Politics, and the Coming of the American Civil War," in Nathan O. Hatch and John H. Wigger, eds., *Methodism and the Shaping of American Culture* (Nashville: Kingswood Books, 2001), 309.

3. Charles Handy, *The Age of Paradox* (Boston: Harvard Business School Press, 1994), 50.

4. Max De Pree, *Leadership Jazz* (New York: Doubleday, 1992), 48.

5. David Halberstam, *October 1964* (New York: Villard Books, 1994), 6.

6. Ibid., 5.

7. Ibid., 5, 14–15.

8. Ibid., 5, 7.

9. Gil Rendle, *Journey in the Wilderness: New Life for Mainline Churches* (Nashville: Abingdon Press, 2010), 64–65.

10. "Thoughts upon Methodism" (1786), in Rupert E. Davies, ed., *The Methodist Societies: History, Nature, and Design,* vol. 9, *The Works of John Wesley,* Bicentennial Edition (Nashville: Abingdon Press, 1989), 527.

1. A New Context

1. "Exploring Off the Map" Conference, Leadership Network, May 23–26, 2000, Broomfield, Colorado.

2. Apparently this is not a new phenomenon. "As the twentieth century dawned, the realization by many leaders of the Methodist Episcopal Church that they were not matching Baptist growth prompted a variety of responses. Some chose to emphasize that receipts from member contributions continued to rise quite rapidly." Roger Finke and Rodney Stark, *The Churching of America 1776–1990: Winners and Losers in Our Religious Economy* (New Brunswick, N.J.: Rutgers University Press, 1992), 166.

3. The figures reported by the General Council on Finance and Administration show a larger figure for the decline because in 2009 money sent to the Women's Division of the General Board of Global Ministries was not included for the first time. The decline in income resulting from this reporting format change is factored out of the calculations used here.

4. The Lewis Center compares the death rates of annual conferences and the denomination with the death rates of those fifteen and older for the respective geographic areas served. This adjustment makes the figures more comparable with church death rates. While some church members are younger than fifteen, this age break is the closest option available from the U.S. Census Bureau statistics.

5. Lovett H. Weems, Jr., and Joe E. Arnold, "Pockets of 'Youthfulness' in an Aging Denomination," Lewis Center for Church Leadership, Wesley Theological Seminary, Spring 2009. Available at www.churchleadership.com/pdfs/Pockets.pdf.

6. Sources for charts and interpretation are U.S. National Center for Health Statistics. *Vital Statistics of the United States,* annual; *National Vital Statistics Reports (NVSR);* and <http://www.cdc.gov/nchs/datawh/statab/unpubd/mortabs/hist293.htm>; Tables 1 and 9, *Projections of the Population and Components of Change for the United States: 2010 to 2050* (NP2008-T1), Population Division, U.S. Census Bureau.

7. The Call to Action initiative came from the Council of Bishops and included research projects leading to reports issued in fall 2010. The basis of the Call to Action Steering Committee report was an OAR prepared by APEX HG LLC and a Vital Congregations Report prepared by Towers Watson. The reports are available at www.umc.org/calltoaction.

8. OAR, 1.

9. For a discussion of "leadership as a channel of God's grace," see Lovett H. Weems, Jr., *Church Leadership: Vision, Team, Culture, and Integrity,* rev. ed. (Nashville: Abingdon Press, 2010), 1–17.

2. Resetting the Financial Baseline

1. Amy Frykholm, "Loose Connections," *Christian Century,* May 31, 2011, 20.

2. OAR, 22.

3. OAR, 29.

4. Gil Rendle calls for a "focus on outcomes" in *Journey in the Wilderness: New Life for Mainline Churches* (Nashville: Abingdon Press, 2010), 99–100. See also Lovett H. Weems, Jr., and Tom Berlin, *Bearing Fruit: Ministry with Real Results* (Nashville: Abingdon Press, 2011).

5. Russell E. Richey, *Methodist Connectionalism: Historical Perspectives* (Nashville: General Board of Higher Education and Ministry, 2009), chapter 8. Richey illustrates with the history of singing "And Are We Yet Alive" at the opening session of annual conference, a tradition going back to about the mid-nineteenth century but hardly back to John Wesley's time, as often proclaimed.

6. "The budget recommendations shall likewise include any other amounts to be apportioned to the districts, charges, or churches by the annual conference for conference or district

causes of any kind." 2008 *Discipline*, paragraph 614.4. One could interpret this provision to exclude approval of district apportionments because they are not technically "apportioned by" the annual conference, though they are certainly apportionments and for "district causes of any kind." Districts sometimes have unions, mission societies, or parsonage funds. Even if approval by the conference is not required, any requests going to churches from the districts for specific amounts for any purpose need to be before the conference Council on Finance and Administration so the congregational impact can include them.

7. Rendle, *Journey in the Wilderness*, 137.

8. *The Journal and Letters of Francis Asbury*, ed. Elmer T. Clark, J. Manning Potts, and Jacob S. Payton (Nashville: Abingdon Press, 1958), 2:593, 613, 615, 643, quoted in John Wigger, *American Saint: Francis Asbury and the Methodists* (New York: Oxford University Press, 2009), 368–69.

9. OAR, 25.

3. General Church

1. OAR, 1.

2. Gil Rendle, *Journey in the Wilderness: New Life for Mainline Churches* (Nashville: Abingdon Press, 2010), 43.

3. See Lovett H. Weems, Jr., *Leadership in the Wesleyan Spirit* (Nashville: Abingdon Press, 1999), chapter 8.

4. Rendle, *Journey in the Wilderness*, 79.

5. See Lovett H. Weems, Jr., *John Wesley's Message Today* (Nashville: Abingdon Press, 1991), introduction.

6. Grant Hagiya, "Foreword," in Russell E. Richey, *Methodist Connectionalism: Historical Perspectives* (Nashville: General Board of Higher Education and Ministry, 2009), xvi.

7. David Hempton, *Methodism: Empire of the Spirit* (New Haven, Conn.: Yale University Press, 2005), 203–4.

8. John H. Wigger, *Taking Heaven by Storm: Methodism and the Rise of Popular Christianity* (New York: Oxford University Press, 1998), 79. Nathan Hatch notes the irony in a hierarchical polity reaching the masses more effectively than the more democratic polities of the time. "The democratization of Christianity, then, has less to do with the specifics of polity and governance and more with the incarnation of the church into popular culture." Nathan O. Hatch, *The Democratization of Christianity* (New Haven, Conn.: Yale University Press, 1989), 9.

9. Wigger, *Taking Heaven by Storm*, 193. See also Scott Kisker, *Mainline or Methodist?: Rediscovering Our Evangelistic Mission* (Nashville: Discipleship Resources, 2008).

10. The continental conferences may give an opportunity to move episcopal elections there without the need for jurisdictional conferences. The continental conferences are a more logical place for such elections than General Conference.

11. OAR, 20.

12. Lyle Schaller, *Tattered Trust: Is There Hope for Your Denomination?* (Nashville: Abingdon Press, 1996), 42.

13. Russell E. Richey and Thomas Edward Frank, *Episcopacy in the Methodist Tradition* (Nashville: Abingdon Press, 2004), 93–94. General oversight of the church's mission is one of four proposals they make.

14. William B. Lawrence captures the challenge faced by the Council of Bishops, on which improvement can be seen since these words appeared. "The true test . . . is whether they can channel their separate gifts into forming a community, a collective body for leadership. Can

they create consensus, where the rest of the church has found only contention? . . . The episcopacy will lead if it offers a new vision of community, transcends pain and prejudice, embraces minority and majority views, manifests the grace of Christian conference, and demonstrates visibly that grace at work." William B. Lawrence, "Episcopacy, Authority, and Leadership," *Circuit Rider*, November 1996, 26.

4. Annual Conference

1. The Constitution of The United Methodist Church, Article II.

2. Russell E. Richey, *Doctrine in Experience: A Methodist Theology of Church and Ministry* (Nashville: Kingswood Books, 2009), 280, from a chapter that appeared initially as "Understandings of Ecclesiology in United Methodism," in *Orthodox and Wesleyan Ecclesiology*, ed. S. T. Kimbrough Jr. (Crestwood, N.Y.: St. Vladimir's Seminary Press, 2007), 149–71.

3. 2008 *Discipline*, paragraph 601.

4. Lovett H. Weems, Jr., *Leadership in the Wesleyan Spirit* (Nashville: Abingdon Press, 1999), see especially chapters 3–4, 10–12.

5. Lyle E. Schaller, *Tattered Trust: Is There Hope for Your Denomination?* (Nashville: Abingdon Press, 1996), 27.

6. "Recent Denominational Research in New Church Development," conducted for Path One, The United Methodist Church, April 2008, Lewis Center for Church Leadership, and Lovett H. Weems, Jr., "Actionable Strategic Insights, New Church Development in The United Methodist Church," April 2008.

7. Nathan O. Hatch, *The Democratization of American Christianity* (New Haven, Conn.: Yale University Press, 1989), 89.

8. Lewis Center for Church Leadership research from denominational and U.S. Census databases.

9. Donald R. House and the staff of RRC, Inc., in Bryan, Texas, and the staff of the Lewis Center for Church Leadership studied all the new church starts between 1985 and 2005 in the state of Texas (Central Texas, North Texas, Northwest Texas, Rio Grande, Southwest Texas, and Texas Conferences) as well as the Virginia and Western North Carolina Conferences.

10. Steering Committee Report and Vital Congregations Report available at www.umc.org/calltoaction.

11. Robert Schnase, *Five Practices of Fruitful Congregations* (Nashville: Abingdon Press, 2007).

12. Even where the United Methodist presence is strong, the increasing number of counties in which no United Methodist church averages one hundred or more in worship means that it is likely that persons moving to that area wanting to join a United Methodist church may not find one with the range of programs they need.

13. This typically happens in small membership churches. My Wesley Seminary colleague Lewis A. Parks has helped the church understand that small churches have been common from the beginning of the church, but they usually have been multigenerational churches. Small churches can remain vital and stable for generations if they are multigenerational. "A Better Script for Small Churches," *Leading Ideas*, online newsletter of the Lewis Center for Church Leadership, www.churchleadership.com, May 26, 2010. See also Lewis A. Parks, *Preaching in the Small Membership Church* (Nashville: Abingdon Press, 2009).

14. Gil Rendle, *Journey in the Wilderness: New Life for Mainline Churches* (Nashville: Abingdon Press, 2010), 137.

5. Congregations

1. Alan J. Roxburgh and Fred Romanuk, *The Missional Leader: Equipping Your Church to Reach a Changing World* (San Francisco: Jossey-Bass, 2006), 45–48. They use the term *performative zone.*

2. Barry A. Kosmin and Ariela Keysar with Ryan Cragun and Juhem Navarro-Rivera, "American Nones: The Profile of the No Religion Population," a report based on the American Religious Identification Survey 2008 (Hartford, Conn.: Program on Public Values, Trinity College, 2009), www.americanreligionsurvey-aris.org/reports/NONES_08.pdf.

3. "U.S. Census Bureau Reports Men and Women Wait Longer to Marry," news release from the U.S. Census Bureau, November 10, 2010.

4. Sam Roberts, "To Be Married Means to Be Outnumbered," *New York Times*, October 15, 2006.

5. David T. Olson, *The American Church in Crisis* (Grand Rapids, Mich.: Zondervan, 2008), 16.

6. "A Nation of Hunkered-Down Homebodies," *New York Times*, January 10, 2010.

7. Amy Frykholm, "Loose Connections," *Christian Century*, May 31, 2011, 20–23. This is not the first time in United Methodist history when not all participants were members. "In 1805 Francis Asbury estimated that membership stood at 100,000, but that up to 1 million people 'regularly attend our ministry.' " John H. Wigger, *Taking Heaven by Storm: Methodism and the Rise of Popular Christianity in America* (New York: Oxford University Press, 1998), 4.

8. "Faith in Flux: Changes in Religious Affiliation in the U.S.," a report from the Pew Forum for Religion and Public Life, April 2009, http://pewforum.org/uploadedfiles/Topics/Religious_Affiliation/fullreport.pdf.

9. Daniel O. Aleshire, "Making Haste Slowly: Celebrating the Future of Theological Schools," *Theological Education* 44, no. 1 (2008): 3.

10. C. Kirk Hadaway and David A. Roozen, *Rerouting the Protestant Mainstream* (Nashville: Abingdon Press, 1995), 114.

11. "The Circumcision of the Heart," in *The Works of John Wesley*, Bicentennial Ed., vol. 1, ed. Albert C. Outler (Nashville: Abingdon Press, 1985), 413.

12. The Lewis Center for Church Leadership compiled the worship attendance statistics from the four denominations referenced. For a more detailed discussion of this worship downturn and possible reasons, see Lovett H. Weems, Jr., "No Shows," *Christian Century*, October 5, 2010, 10–11.

13. Albert C. Outler, *Evangelism in the Wesleyan Spirit* (Nashville: Tidings, 1971), 103.

14. For more on this topic see Lovett H. Weems, Jr., *Leadership in the Wesleyan Spirit* (Nashville: Abingdon Press, 1999), chapters 3 and 4.

6. Reaching More People, Younger People, More Diverse People

1. Lovett H. Weems, Jr., "Ten Provocative Questions for The United Methodist Church." This was one of several presentations to the Council of Bishops in November 2007 in response to the State of the Church research report issued in the spring of 2007.

2. Whites make up 80 percent of the age sixty-five and older population and, on the other end of the age spectrum, only about half of babies under the age of two. "More Minority Babies Being Born in U.S.," Associated Press, June 24, 2011.

3. Hope Yen and John Raby, "Census Estimates Show 1 in 4 Counties Are Dying," Associated Press, February 11, 2011.

4. Figures for professions of faith in the chart include two groups of people—those joining by profession of faith and those reported as "restored" to membership.

5. "A Survey of United Methodist Laity and Clergy," October 23, 2006, 50, 53. This is the quantitative report from the State of the Church research project conducted by the Connectional Table and is available at www.umc.org/atf/cf/%7BDB6A45E4-C446-4248-82C8-E131B6424741%7D/CTQuantitativeFinal.pdf.

6. Erwin McManus, *Rapid Advance: Core Values, Awaken CD*, 2006.

7. "Clergy Age Trends in The United Methodist Church, 1985–2011," Lewis Center for Church Leadership, Wesley Theological Seminary, 2010. Article is available at www.church leadership.com. The challenge is heightened by the fact that in 2011 more than 50 percent of active elders are between the ages of fifty-five and seventy-two, a record high, with the most common retirement age recently being sixty-four. The median age of fifty-five in 2010 and 2011 is the highest in history, up from fifty in 2000 and forty-five in 1973.

8. Ann A. Michel and Lovett H. Weems, Jr., *The Crisis of Younger Clergy* (Nashville: Abingdon Press, 2008).

9. Adam Hamilton, *When Christians Get It Wrong* (Nashville: Abingdon Press, 2010).

10. Christian Smith and Melissa Lundquist Denton in *Soul Searching: The Religious and Spiritual Lives of American Teenagers* (Oxford: Oxford University Press, 2005), Kenda Creasy Dean, *Almost Christian: What the Faith of Our Teenagers Is Telling the American Church* (Oxford: Oxford University Press, 2010), Kenda Creasy Dean, *Practicing Passion: Youth and the Quest for a Passionate Church* (Grand Rapids: Eerdmans, 2004), and Carol E. Lytch, *Choosing Church: What Makes a Difference for Teens* (Louisville: Westminster John Knox, 2004). Two articles that summarize these findings are Ann A. Michel, "Making Church Matter for Youth," *Leading Ideas* (Lewis Center for Church Leadership), July 6, 2005, and Jessicah Duckworth, "Cultivating a Consequential Faith in Adolescents," *Leading Ideas* (Lewis Center for Church Leadership), January 11, 2011.

11. Smith and Denton, *Soul Searching*.

12. William H. Frey, "Five Myths about the 2010 Census and the U.S. Population," *Washington Post*, February 14, 2010.

13. "Reaching More Diverse People in The United Methodist Church," Lewis Center for Church Leadership, Wesley Theological Seminary, June 1, 2011. Joe E. Arnold was research manager for the project for the Lewis Center. This project was done in partnership with John H. Southwick of the Research Office, General Board of Global Ministries, using membership data maintained by the General Council on Finance and Administration. Since 1989 congregations have reported membership by racial ethnic background. The report presents a snapshot of United Methodism's efforts through 2009 to reach more racially diverse people in the United States.

14. John H. Southwick, "Background Data for Mission," General Board of Global Ministries, August 2005.

15. At the same time this Southwick analysis was done, another researcher, Donald R. House, was looking at the same issue but using counties instead of zip codes. He listed all U.S. counties in declining order by MHI and then attributed United Methodist membership based

on the location of churches within their respective counties. The same pattern appeared of highest United Methodist presence in the top cohort of counties and gradual decline in presence in each group of counties from wealthiest to poorest.

16. Penny Long Marler, "Lost in the Fifties: The Changing Family and the Nostalgic Church," in *Work, Family, and Religion in Contemporary Society*, ed. Nancy Tatom Ammerman and Wade Clark Roof (New York: Routledge, 1995), 25.

17. "The Decline of Marriage and Rise of New Families," Pew Research Center, November 18, 2010, http://pewresearch.org/pubs/1802/decline-marriage-rise-new-families; "U.S. Census Bureau Reports Men and Women Wait Longer to Marry," November 10, 2010, www.census.gov/newsroom/releases/archives/families_households/cb10-174.html

Conclusion

1. Walter Brueggemann, *Cadences of Home: Preaching among Exiles* (Louisville: Westminster John Knox, 1997), 133.

2. Bruce C. Birch, *Let Justice Roll Down* (Louisville: Westminster John Knox, 1991), 293.

3. For more on the importance of hope and perseverance to leadership, see Lovett H. Weems, Jr., *Take the Next Step: Leading Lasting Change in the Church* (Nashville: Abingdon Press, 2003), chapter 8.

4. Russell E. Richey, *Methodist Connectionalism: Historical Perspectives* (Nashville: General Board of Higher Education and Ministry, 2009), 246.

5. William Warren Sweet, *The American Churches: An Interpretation* (London: Epworth Press, 1947), 18.

CPSIA information can be obtained at www.ICGtesting.com
Printed in the USA
LVOW011827291211

261578LV00001B/1/P